CAMBRIDGE PRIMARY
English

Learner's Book

3

Gill Budgell and Kate Ruttle

CAMBRIDGE
UNIVERSITY PRESS

CAMBRIDGE
UNIVERSITY PRESS

University Printing House, Cambridge CB2 8BS, United Kingdom

Cambridge University Press is part of the University of Cambridge.

It furthers the University's mission by disseminating knowledge in the pursuit of education, learning and research at the highest international levels of excellence.

Information on this title: education.cambridge.org

First published 2015

Printed in India by Replika Press Pvt. Ltd

A catalogue record for this publication is available from the British Library

ISBN 978-1-107-63282-0 Paperback

Contents

Welcome to the *Cambridge Primary English* Series, Stage 3.

This Learner's Book will take you through Stage 3 of the Cambridge Primary curriculum. It has nine units of lessons and activities to help you with your speaking and listening skills, reading skills and writing skills. Other activities will develop your practical skills.

These icons will show you how you're going to work:

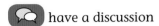 have a discussion

do some reading

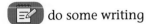 do some writing

act, sing, make things and play games

AZ do a spelling activity

Three units in the book are about fiction:

- Unit 1, *Ordinary days*, has stories about real life
- Unit 4, *Fiery beginnings*, has myths, legends and fables about fire
- Unit 7, *Dragons and pirates*, introduces some adventure stories.

Three units are about non-fiction:

- Unit 2, *Let's have a party!*, is about instruction texts
- Unit 5, *Letters*, looks at different reasons people write to each other
- Unit 8, *Wonderful world*, looks at information texts about places.

There are also three units are about rhymes and poetry:

- Unit 3, *See, hear, feel, enjoy*, has plays and poems about the senses
- Unit 6, *Poems from around the world*, has poems that describe places and countries
- Unit 9, *Laughing allowed*, looks at jokes, funny poems and ways of playing with words.

In every unit look out for these features too:

Hello! I am here to guide and help you.

Tip

These tips give you handy hints as you work.

Did you know?

These boxes provide interesting information and opportunities for further research.

How did I do?

These boxes help you check your own progress along the way.

Language focus

These boxes will explain specific language rules.

On pages 127 to 133 you'll find interesting and enjoyable spelling rules and activities to practise and expand your knowledge of spelling. You can go there whenever you like to check your own spelling skills or to learn more about common spelling patterns and letter strings.

On pages 134 to 143 you'll find a Toolkit – a set of resources for you to use at any time. These include tools and tips such as an editing checklist, a self-evaluation tool for reading aloud and a list of group work rules.

We hope you enjoy the course and that it helps you feel confident about responding to English, and using English in a variety of ways.

Gill Budgell and Kate Ruttle

1 Ordinary days

In this unit you will look at stories that are about children like you. You will learn about settings and characters, and you will learn how to make your reading sound interesting. At the end of the unit you will write your own story.

You will also learn about:
nouns, verbs and adjectives,
dialogue in stories.

1 Setting the scene

A 💬 AZ Talk about places

1. Look at the pictures. What are the places you can see?
2. Have you visited any of these places? Ask and answer the following questions:
   - What did you do there?
   - Why were you there?
   - Did you enjoy being there?
   - Did anything interesting happen to you there?

B ✏️ **We use nouns and adjectives when we write stories.**

1 Think of nouns and adjectives for the six pictures A–F.

2 In your notebook write six sentences, one for each picture. Describe each one with a noun and an adjective. Remember to use a capital letter at the beginning of each sentence and a full stop at the end.

It is a busy classroom.

I have a messy bedroom.

Language focus

Nouns are words we use to name things. For example, the words *house, bed, shop, beach, hill* and *flower* are nouns.

Adjectives are words we use to describe nouns. For example, the words *big, small, pretty, lovely, nice, dirty, horrible, high* and *low* are adjectives.

C 💬 **Stories have settings. The setting includes a description** of the place, like your sentences in Activity B.

It can also include information about:

- the weather (e.g. *in a noisy thunderstorm*)
- the time (e.g. *When Arturo was a little boy …*).

1 Choose one of the **settings** you wrote in Activity B.

2 Talk about a story or adventure that could happen in your chosen setting.

You have just written six settings for a story!

Did you know?

The author Roald Dahl used lots of different settings in his books for children. He wrote them all in a shed in his back garden!

2 An ordinary school day

Once upon an ordinary school day, an ordinary boy woke from his ordinary dreams, got out of his ordinary bed, had ... an ordinary wash, put on his ordinary clothes and ate his ordinary breakfast.

The ordinary boy brushed his ordinary teeth, kissed his ordinary mum goodbye and set off for his ordinary school.

A 📖 ⭐ **Look at the opening of a story called *Once Upon an Ordinary School Day*.**

1 Read the opening of the story.
2 Now re-read the opening aloud to a talk partner. Can you read it in an interesting way so that your partner wants to keep on listening?

Any volunteers?
Look again at the first sentence of *Once upon an Ordinary School Day*. Find all the words which contain the letter **o**. Read them aloud. How many different ways do you pronounce the letter **o** in the first sentence?

Tip

If you're stuck on how to read a word, try the following strategies:

- Sound it out. Remember to look through the whole word for spelling patterns you know. For example, the word *clothes* has o_e so the **o** is long.

- Divide it into syllables. For example, the word *ordinary* can be split into four syllables: *or-di-na-ry*.

- Match it to other words you know. For example, *once* is like *one*, and the **o** is said the same way.

Tip

Look at the letter **o** by itself and as part of different letter patterns in the words.

B 📝 💬 **AZ** **Check your understanding.**

1 Answer these questions in your notebook.
   a What was the boy doing before he woke up?
   b What did he do just before he put his clothes on?
   c What did he do after he kissed his mum?

2 Talk about the story opening.
   a What does the writer want you to know about the boy?
   b What kind of story do you think this is going to be?
   c What might happen in the story?

3 The power of words

The ordinary boy went into his ordinary classroom and sat at his ordinary desk. Then, something quite out of the ordinary happened …

"Good morning, everybody!" said a quite extraordinary figure, bounding into the classroom. "My name is Mr Gee and I'm your new teacher. Now, you don't know me and I don't know you, so, to help me to get to know you, I've had an idea …"

As Mr Gee handed out paper, he said, "For our first lesson together I want you to listen to some music and I want you to let the music make pictures in your heads. Is that clear?"

And the ordinary children whispered: "He's barmy!" "He's bonkers!" "He's as nutty as a fruitcake!" "Music?" "Pictures?" "What's he on about?"

And Mr Gee said, "Shush, just close your eyes, open your ears and listen."

And the music began: a rumbling, rolling, <u>thunderous</u> music that boomed and crashed around the classroom.

Suddenly it stopped. And Mr Gee said: "Tell me what the music made you think of."

One girl shouted, "Stampeding horses!"

Someone else said, "No, it was racing cars!"

And the ordinary boy said, "I saw elephants, Sir, and there were hundreds of them!"

"Yes," laughed Mr Gee. "Isn't it wonderful? Now, I want all of you to try to put what you hear on paper. Start writing!"

And as the music grew and swooped and danced and dived once more, the ordinary boy began to write.

By Colin McNaughton

A 📖 📝 **What happens to the ordinary boy? Read what happens next in the story and answer these questions in your notebook.**

1 Who was the *quite extraordinary figure*?
2 What was the first thing the children had to do?
3 What helped the children while they were writing?

B **Discuss these questions.**

1 Did the story continue how you thought it would?
2 What made the change happen?
3 What has changed for the ordinary boy?
4 What do you think might happen next?

Any volunteers?
Have you ever made pictures in your head while listening to music? If not, try it! Music without words is best.

Language focus

Remember that adjectives are words that describe things.
Adjectives can go either before a noun or after it.

He   is   an   ordinary   boy.
                      ↑   ↑
                 adjective   noun

The   boy   is   ordinary.
        ↑   ↑
      noun   adjective

C AZ **Look at the way adjectives are used in the story. Before Mr Gee arrives the only adjective used is _ordinary_. But when he arrives there's a new adjective: _extraordinary_.**

1 Find all the adjectives in the story after Mr Gee arrives. How many adjectives are there?
2 Why does the author suddenly use all these interesting words?
3 Find the underlined word _thunderous_ in the story. What do you think it means?
4 Look up these adjectives in your dictionary. Write the words and their meanings in your notebook.

> bonkers   rumbling   stampeding

Tip

If you don't know what a word means:

• think of other words that look and sound a bit the same, for example _thunderous_ sounds like _thunder_

• read the rest of the sentence and see if you can work it out

• look up the word in a dictionary.

Look at the two pictures of a car park near a shopping mall.

1 Decide what is the same and what is different in the two pictures.

2 Look at these adjectives. Which picture does each one describe?

> sad cheerful sunny dark rainy warm stormy
> bright dull empty colourful busy dangerous
> smiley lively thundery gloomy light happy

3 Write three sentences to describe the setting in each of the pictures –
   it can be the place, the weather or the time. Remember that adjectives
   can go before or after a noun.

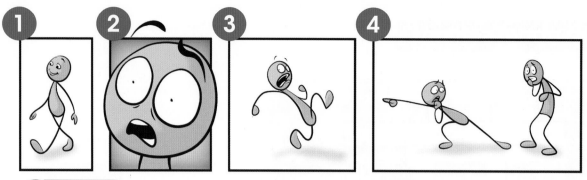

B 💬 📝 Create a setting and use it in a story.

1   Look at the cartoon strip. What do you think has happened?
    What do you think the setting is? Does the cartoon strip tell a story?

2   Think of a title for the cartoon strip story.

3   Write a description of the setting using interesting words.

5 Characters

A 💬 📝 **AZ** We usually want to know four things about the characters
in a story:

- what they look like
- what they do
- what they think or say
- how they feel.

1   Look back at the cartoon strip in the last session. Tell the story to a talk
    partner. Remember to include information about the setting. Give each of
    the characters a name. Include some information about them too.

2   Write a description of the main character using interesting words to make
    him or her come to life.

B 💬 📝 Create another character.

1   Look at the three illustrations. Who would you most like to be friends with?
    Why?

Juan

Asibi

Liang

2 Think of an adjective to describe each of the three characters. Write your three adjectives in your notebook.

3 Read the character portrait of Liang. Do you think these statements are true or false?

Liang hangs out in the mall with his friends. He and his friends usually wear earplugs so they have to SMS each other if they want to talk. Sometimes Liang texts back; sometimes he doesn't.

Liang is interested in computers. He enjoys flicking through websites, finding out about the latest improvements and new releases. He and his friends mostly communicate through SMS and online. When they visit the mall, they generally saunter over to a computer shop to examine the computers on display.

   a Liang and his friends have fun together.
   b Liang talks a lot.
   c Liang knows a lot about computers.
   d Liang is excited about visiting the computer shop.
   e Liang likes playing football.

4 In your notebook write a character portrait of either Juan or Asibi. Include information about:
- what Juan/Asibi likes doing
- the kind of person he/she is.

6 Verbs

Language focus

Verbs tell you what someone or something does, is or has.

Verbs also tell you when the action in the sentence happens:

When?	What?	Tense
Yesterday morning	she **walked** to school.	past
Every morning	she **walks** to school.	present
Tomorrow morning	she **will walk** to school.	future

A sentence must:

● have a verb – if there isn't a verb, it isn't a sentence
● begin with a capital letter
● end with a full stop, question mark or exclamation mark
● make sense.

Verbs are sometimes called 'doing' words, but they are also 'being' or 'having' words.

Did you know?

The verb *be* is the most common verb in the English language. Different parts of the verb are tricky to recognise. They include the little words *am, is, are, was* and *were*.

A **AZ** Decide which of the following are sentences. Write the sentences in your notebook and underline the verb in each one.

1 The cute kittens.
2 She whispered to her friend.
3 I love chocolate.
4 I heard hundreds of elephants.
5 Some dangerous sharks.
6 They walk to school together.

No verb? Not a sentence!

B  Write these sentences in your notebook, completing each one with the correct form of the verb *be*.

1 When he ... six, Liang could play the piano very well.
2 His fingers ... very good at finding the notes.
3 Now that Liang ... eight, he can mend computers.
4 Liang's teacher says that he ... very clever.
5 "I ... very interested in computers," said Liang.

C These sentences all contain a form of the verb *have*. Write the sentences in your notebook. Then find the different forms of *have* and underline them.

1 Sharks have sharp teeth.
2 I had a toy like that when I was little.
3 She is having a violin lesson at the moment.
4 She has no front teeth at the moment.

Tip

Different forms of a verb often look a bit like each other. Try looking for words that begin with the same letters as **ha**ve.

7 Amazing Grace

1 Grace was a girl who loved stories. She didn't mind if they were read to her or told to her or made up out of her own head. She didn't care if they were from books or on TV or in films or on the video or out of Nana's long memory. Grace just loved stories. And after she had heard them, or sometimes while they were still going on, Grace would act them out. And she always gave herself the most exciting part.

2 One day at school her teacher said they were going to do the play of *Peter Pan*. Grace put up her hand to be … Peter Pan.

"You can't be called Peter," said Raj. "That's a boy's name."

But Grace kept her hand up.

"You can't be Peter Pan," whispered Natalie. "He wasn't black." But Grace kept her hand up.

"All right," said the teacher. "Lots of you want to be Peter Pan, so we'll have to have auditions. We'll choose the parts next Monday."

3 When Grace got home, she seemed rather sad.

"What's the matter?" asked Ma.

"Raj said I couldn't be Peter Pan because I'm a girl."

"That just shows all Raj knows about it," said Ma. "Peter Pan is *always* a girl!"

Grace cheered up, then later she remembered something else. "Natalie says I can't be Peter Pan because I'm black," she said.

Ma started to get angry but Nana stopped her.

"It seems that Natalie is another one who don't know nothing," she said.

"You can be anything you want, Grace, if you put your mind to it."

A 💬 📖 **AZ** **This text is from a story called *Amazing Grace* by Mary Hoffman.**

1 What do you think the word *amazing* means? Talk about what it might mean.

2 Read the story extract. (The paragraphs are numbered to help you talk about the story later.)

B 💬 📝 **Explore the meaning of the story.**

1 Discuss the last phrase of the extract, *if you put your mind to it*. What do you think it means? Does Nana think that Grace could be Peter Pan?

2 Answer these questions in your notebook.

   a What did Grace like most?

   b What was going to happen in school?

   c Which part did Grace want to be?

   d Why was Grace sad when she got home?

3 Discuss the story so far.

    a What do we know about Grace, Ma and Nana?

    b What are the settings?

    c How do you think the story will finish? Give your reasons.

4 What is the **theme** (the main idea) of the story? Look at what some other children said was the theme. Which one do you think is the best answer? What do you think is the theme?

A It's fun to act out stories.

B Lots of people want the main part in a play, but only one person can have it.

C If you put your mind to it, you can be anything you want to be.

D Grace liked acting so she got the best part in the play.

8 Dialogue

A 🗨 There is lots of dialogue (talking) in the text on page 16. How do we know what the characters say to each other in the story? Re-read part 2 of the extract.

1 How many people talk in this part of the story?

2 Who are they?

3 What are the words that Natalie says to Grace?

4 How do you know Natalie is talking?

> **Tip**
>
> When you are looking for what people say, look for speech marks before and after the words people say, like this: "Thank you!"

B 📖 ★ **AZ** When you write dialogue, you use a verb to show that a character said something. But don't use the verb *said* each time – that would be boring!

1 Re-read the whole story. Which other words are used instead of *said*? Think of a different verb the writer could have used instead of *said*.

2 Read these sentences aloud with expression to a talk partner. Use the verb to work out how to say the words. Talk about how and why you changed your voice.

- "Good morning," he said.
- "Good morning," she mumbled.
- "Good morning," he yelled.
- "Good morning," she sobbed.
- "Good morning," he whispered.

> The verbs give a lot of information about how the characters are feeling when they speak. We start a new line for each new character.

9 Sequencing events

A 💬 **Discuss the sequence, or order, of the main events of the story.**

1 Work in a group to decide the order these events happened in.

A The auditions happen in school.

B Grace is a great success in the play.

C Some children tell her she can't be Peter Pan but Nana says she can do anything.

D She wants to be Peter Pan.

E Grace likes acting out stories.

F All the children vote for Grace because she is the best Peter Pan.

2 Now use the six main events from question 1 to make a story mountain. Talk about where each event should go. Copy the diagram into your notebook.

4 Exciting part

3 Development   5 Then what happens?

2 Beginning / Problem

1 Introduction   6 Ending

Did you know?

The story mountain shows the shape of most stories. You can use it to plan your own stories or to understand the events in a story you have read.

B ⭐ **Act out the story.**

1 Decide who will play the different characters in the story.

2 Act out the story using your story mountain.

 **Think of an idea for a new story and make a plan.**

1   Discuss ideas for a new story based on the pattern of *Amazing Grace*.
    Choose one of your ideas to write about.

2   Draw a story mountain in your notebook and plot the main events of
    your story.

3   Write some notes about the setting and characters at the side of your
    story mountain. Your story mountain and notes will be your plan.

Eduardo wants to be in the football
team. Jorge says he's too small.

If you're stuck for ideas for
your story, how about one
of these suggestions?

Viktoria wants to ride in a pony show.
Olivia says she can't ride well enough.

Tim wants to drive a go-kart. His dad is
worried he might get hurt.

B 🗨 **A-Z** Tell your story.

1 Tell your story to yourself first. Remember to include some dialogue.

2 Now tell it to a talk partner. Ask your partner to tell you something you could do to make your story better.

3 Change your story plan to include any new ideas you or your talk partner had about your story.

11 Write a story

A 🗨 📝 Tell your story again to a talk partner so that you know what to write. Then write your story, following your plan. Remember to include:

- a setting
- a description of the character or characters
- some dialogue.

B 📝 Check your handwriting.

Good handwriting helps your reader to enjoy your story. Is your handwriting a good size, with regular spaces between the letters and between the words?

12 Improve your story

A 📖 Re-read the story that you wrote in the last session. Have you followed your plan? Do you need to add some dialogue?

B 📝 Could your descriptions be even better?

1 Look again at your descriptions of the setting and the main character. Add three adjectives to improve each of the descriptions.

2 Re-read your story and check it carefully for any errors. Check:
- the grammar
- the spelling
- the punctuation.

How did I do?

C 💬 In this unit you have read or listened to parts of *Once Upon an Ordinary Day* and *Amazing Grace*. Talk about what was the same about the stories and what was different. Which story did you like best? Why?

D 📝 You have learned about nouns, verbs and adjectives, and about dialogue in stories.

1 Copy the table into your notebook and write these words in the table.

> ball   bounced   black   smiled   silly   school   quick   queen   quacked

Nouns	Verbs	Adjectives

2 Look at these sentences about dialogue. Which ones are true?
Copy the true sentences in your notebook.

   a We use the word *dialogue* to talk about silly things people do.

   b We use the word *dialogue* to talk about conversations in stories.

   c We put speech marks around words like "he said" so we know who is talking.

   d We put speech marks around the words characters say so we know what they said.

   e We start a new paragraph when a new character says something.

   f We start a new line when a new character says something.

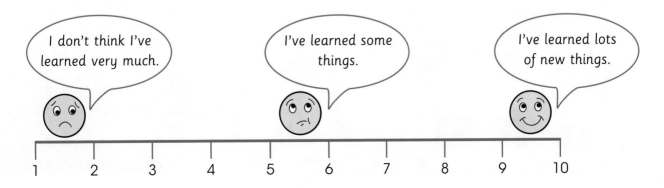

I don't think I've learned very much.

I've learned some things.

I've learned lots of new things.

1   2   3   4   5   6   7   8   9   10

2 Let's have a party!

In this unit you will learn about instructions and invitations. You will read different sorts of instructions and write your own instructions as you plan for a class party.

You will also learn about:

command verbs and sequencing words, tenses, prefixes and suffixes, compound words, adjectives and adverbs.

1 Celebrations

Language focus

To read the word *celebrations* you can:

- split it into syllables – *ce-le-bra-tions*
- look for words and suffixes – *celebration* has the verb *celebrate* plus the suffix **tion**, making the verb into a noun.
- Look at the words in the table.

Verb	Noun
celebrate	celebration
invite	invitation
instruct	instruction
prepare	preparation

A

B

C

D

E

F

A 🗨 AZ Talk about different celebrations.

1 Talk about the photos on page 22. Which celebrations do they show?

2 Talk about a celebration you have been to.

B 📖 AZ Find out about celebrations.

Use a dictionary to find the definition of *celebration*. Do a search on the internet and look at books to find out more.

When you tell someone about something you have done, remember to say:
- **why** you were celebrating
- **what** you did
- **where** you were
- **when** it happened
- **who** else was there.

Tip

You need to know the alphabet to use a dictionary. Check you know it!

A B C D E F G H I J K L M
N O P Q R S T U V W X Y Z

2 A class party

A 🗨 📝 Let's plan a party for the class!

1 What is a party? Talk about:
- what you need to do before the party
- how you will tell people there is a party
- what you could do at the party.

2 Make a list of the ideas you have discussed.

B 📝 Can you remember what you learned about verbs in Unit 1?

Copy these sentences into your notebook.
Underline the verb in each one.

1 Write ideas for a class party.

2 Some people dance at parties.

3 Parties are fun.

4 Make invitations for a class party.

Any volunteers?
Who remembers what verbs are?
Look back at the **Language focus** box on page 14 if you need to.

3 Fiction or non-fiction?

Did you know?

We can use special words to talk about different kinds of writing.

text	=	any piece of writing
fiction	=	a story or text that someone has made up
non-fiction	=	a text giving information or telling the reader true things
text type	=	a particular kind of text – either fiction (e.g. traditional tales or fantasy stories) or non-fiction (e.g. instructions, explanations).

A **AZ** **Is it fiction or non-fiction? Look at some books and decide whether they are fiction or non-fiction. How do you know?**

Tip

If you don't know whether a book is fiction or non-fiction, try these steps to help you decide.

1 Look at the title. The titles of non-fiction books usually tell you what the book is about; fiction books may have a more imaginative title.

2 Look at the pictures on the cover. Non-fiction books may have photographs or realistic pictures.

3 Read the blurb. The blurb on the back cover tells you the subject of the book if it is non-fiction, or what the story is about if it is fiction.

4 Flick through the book. Does it have a contents page or index? Are there headings above short paragraphs of writing? If so, it's probably a non-fiction book.

B **Look at texts 1–3 on page 25. Are they fiction or non-fiction?**

1 Read the texts. Which is an invitation? Which is a story? Which is instructions?

2 Talk about the differences between the texts. Talk about the features of each type.

3 Make a list of the main features of each text type in your notebook.

1

A surprise for Vovó

João was excited.
Vovó was going to be eighty and the family was
planning to have a surprise party for her. He had known
his grandmother was old, but not that old. He wondered what
old people did at parties. They couldn't dance or play games.
Perhaps they just ate and talked. Suddenly, he felt less excited. But this was
going to be a surprise party. He wondered what he could do to surprise her.

How to make a sponge cake

2

You will need:
175 g softened butter, sugar and flour
3 medium eggs
1 tsp baking powder

What to do:
1 First mix together the butter and the sugar.
2 Add the eggs and beat until smooth
   and creamy.
3 Now mix the baking powder in with the flour.
4 Then sift the flour into the butter mix and
   gently fold in.
5 Finally spoon the mixture into two shallow
   cake tins and bake in a medium oven for
   25 minutes.

3

Amelia

is invited to
Vovó's Surprise Party.
It will be at
Santa Teresa Colombo Café
Rio de Janeiro
on 18th May at 4.30.
Come dressed to impress.
RSVP

The **features** of a text type are
the things that make that text
type different from the others.
The features include the **purpose**
of a text, its **layout** and the
language used in it.

 Answer these questions in your notebook.

1 What does João want to do at Vovó's party?
2 When you make this cake, what must you do after you beat the eggs?
3 In which city will Vovó's party be held?

A 💬 📝 ★ **AZ** **Continue planning the class party.**

1 Talk about the party you are planning for the class.

- Who will be at the party?
- Will the party have a theme?
- Will you need to prepare invitations? Why?

How to make a pop-up card

You will need:

3 pieces of card:
- Card 1: 25 cm (10″) long 20 cm (8″) wide
- Card 2: 12 cm (5″) long 8 cm (3″) wide
- Card 3: 12 cm (5″) square

- scissors
- a ruler
- glue
- colouring pens or pencils

How to make the pop-up card:

1 First fold Card 1 in half

2 Then draw a line 1 cm (½″) from either end of Card 2.

3 Fold Card 2 along both the lines, then fold it in half.

4 Next open Card 1.

5 Glue along the ends of Card 2, then stick Card 2 inside Card 1, as shown in the diagram.

6 Draw a party picture on Card 3 and cut it out.

7 Finally glue your party picture onto the edge of Card 2.

2 Look at the *How to make a pop-up card* text. What sort of text is it? Read the text and talk about its features.

3 Now follow the instructions for making a pop-up card.

4 When you have finished, put your card somewhere safe – you will need it in the next session.

B 📝 Good instructions are clear and easy to follow. The sentences have a special form of the verb.

1 Look again at the instructions for making a pop-up card. Find all the verbs. Where are they in the sentence? Write a list of the verbs in your notebook.

2 Now find all the other words at the beginning of the sentences. Make a list of these words in your notebook too.

Language focus

The form of the verb used in instruction texts is sometimes called a **command verb** because it tells, or commands, you to do something, such as *draw*, *open* or *fold*.

Words such as *first*, *next* and *finally* tell you the order to do things in. They are called **sequencing words**.

Instructions usually begin with a command verb or a sequencing word.

5 Write an invitation

C 💬 📝 **AZ** Write an invitation to your class party. First look again at the party invitation on page 25.

1 Talk about the invitation. Whose party is it?

2 Talk about when the party takes place. Has it happened yet? How do you know? Which words give you that information?

3 Look at the **Language focus** box. Then copy and fill in the table.

Past tense	Present tense	Future tense
happened	happens	will happen
enjoyed		will enjoy
	laughs	will laugh
danced		

Language focus

The form of the verb helps you understand the time of an event. It tells you if the event is in the past, the present or the future. These different forms are called **tenses**.

B How do you know the text on page 25 is an invitation?

1 Talk about the layout – where the writing is on the page.
Why isn't it all on one line?

2 Discuss the order the information is given in.

3 What other information is included in the invitation? What does
RSVP (*répondez s'il vous plaît*) mean?

4 Discuss the important information you need to include
in your invitations. Make a list in your notebook.

Remember to use capital letters and full stops!

C You're now ready to write your invitation.

1 First find the pop-up card you made in the last session.

2 Use a computer to write your invitation.
Think about the layout and the order you give the information in.

3 When you have written your invitation, print it and cut it out.
Then stick it on the front of your pop-up card.

6 More instructions

 A There are lots of different types of instructions.

1 Read these instruction texts, 1–4. They are all the beginning of longer texts.

2 What is the purpose of each text?

3 Make a list of features of these instruction texts.

1

Birthday party rules

- Listen when people are telling you about the game.
- Try not to argue.
- Remember to share.

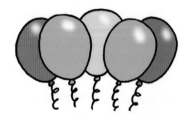

2

How to make a model car

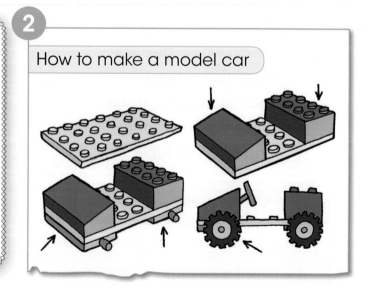

3

Making a paper aeroplane

First fold a piece of paper from end to end along the middle.

Then carefully fold back two corners to make a point.

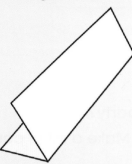

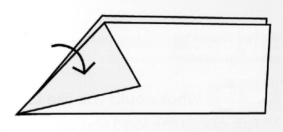

4

How to make dulce de leche:

1 Fill a large saucepan with water and heat until it boils.

2 Put your tin of condensed milk into the water. Allow to simmer for two hours.

Always ask an adult to help you with cooking.

C  **What are compound words?**

1 Look at these words. What do you notice about them?

> saucepan   birthday   something   everyone   layout   notebook

2 Did you notice that they are all **compound words** – words made up from two other words? Look at these words. Make compound words from them and write them in your notebook.

> hair   bed   bath   brush   room   play   band   tooth   paste   time

Tip

Be aware of compound words when you're reading – it can make long words easier to read. Look for words with unusual strings of consonants, for example *bookcase*, *seatbelt*, *popcorn* and *cupboard*. Compound words are easy to spell – you just spell the two shorter words one after the other.

3 Now look at these words. Make some more compound words and write them in your notebook.

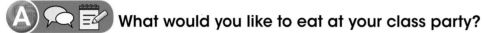

every   any   thing   one   some   no   where   how   body

7 Party food

 What would you like to eat at your class party?

1 Talk about the food you could have at your party. Make a list of party food in your notebook.

2 What kind of book would tell you how to make the food? Where could you find the book?

1

Fruit rockets

You will need:

- A slice of watermelon, about 1 cm (½") thick
- 2 strawberries
- Half a small banana
- A slice of pineapple
- 3 wooden skewers

Method:

1 First cut the watermelon into 3 triangles. Cut the top point off each triangle.
2 Push a piece of watermelon onto a skewer. This is the base of your rocket.
3 Next cut the strawberries in half.
4 Push half a strawberry onto the skewer, above the watermelon.
5 Then cut down the middle of the banana. Cut off slices about 2cm long and thread them onto the skewer above the strawberry.
6 Finally cut the pineapple slice into triangles. Place a triangle, point up, at the top of the rocket.
7 Make two more rockets.
8 Serve immediately.

(31)

 **Look at text 1.**

1 What type of text is text 1? How do you know? What sort of book does the page come from?

2 Discuss what is the same and what is different about texts 2 and 3. When would you use each page? Which book do they come from?

3 Look again at the list of food you made in Activity A. Find some recipes in books and on the internet for party snacks and add one or two items to your list of party food. Make a note of where you found the recipes.

2 Contents

Healthy drinks

Nutty banana whirl	28
Orange refresher	28
Honey and yoghurt smoothie	29

Healthy snacks

Fruit rockets	31
Orange oat biscuits	32
Carrot slice	33

3 Index

8 Lists

A You've decided to make fruit rockets using the recipe on page 30 but you don't have everything you need. Don't worry, you can go shopping!

1 Write a list of the ingredients you need to buy. Think about the layout of your list.

2 Rewrite your list in alphabetical order.

3 Look at your list of party food ideas from the last session. Choose one of the snacks on your list and find the recipe you need to make it.

4 Which ingredients do you need to buy? Write a shopping list.

Make sure you know the English alphabet!
A B C D E F G H I J K L M N O P Q R S T U V W X Y Z

B 💬 📝 **AZ** Look at these words.

> agree   popular   do   like   zip
> honest   tie   please   lucky   happy
> qualify   tidy   usual   obey

1 Try adding the prefix **dis** or **un** to the words.
   What happens? Can you see that the new word means
   the opposite of the one you started with?

2 Copy and fill in the table in your notebook, adding **dis** or **un** to the
   words above. Check you understand the meaning of the words.

Words with **dis**	Words with **un**
distrust	uncover

> *Be careful with spellings! You may have to double one of the letters.*

C 📝 **AZ** Now think about the suffixes **y** and **ly**.

1 Look at these words.

> quick   bad   wind   mess   kind   mud   clear   clean   cloud   dirt   real   sleep

2 Draw another table in your notebook with the headings 'Words with **y**' and
   'Words with **ly**'. Fill it in with the words in the box, adding **y** or **ly** to the end
   of each one. Check you understand the meaning of the words.

Words with **y**	Words with **ly**
thirsty	slowly

Language focus

When you add **y** to the end of a word you turn a noun into an adjective.
Adjectives give you more information about a noun.
When you add **ly** to the end of some words you turn an adjective into an
adverb. **Adverbs** give you more information about a verb. They can tell you
when the action is done or how it is done.

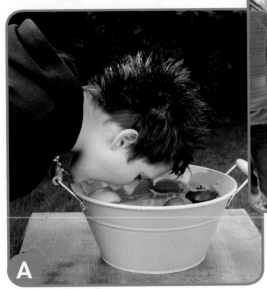

A 💬 📝 **AZ** **What are you going to do at the class party?**

1 What are these children doing at their parties?
What do you like doing at parties? Playing games?
Decide what you would like to do at your class party.

2 Look again at the different types of instructions in this unit.
In your notebook write a list of everything you need to remember
when you write instructions.

- In a different colour pen, underline everything that would be the
  same if you spoke rather than wrote the instructions.
- In another colour pen, add anything that you'd do differently if
  people could only hear your instructions and not read them.

Any volunteers?
Why not write some
rules for working
together in a group?

B ⭐ **Practise giving some
instructions for a simple game.
Think about how you speak when
you give instructions.**

Tip

Speak clearly. Make sure people can
hear you – don't speak too quietly
or too fast.

10 Plan a game

A 💬 📝 **Invent a party game!**

1 Talk about how you could change or improve a party game you already know.

2 Plan the party game. Make notes in your notebook about how to play the new game.
   - What equipment do you need?
   - How many people can play?
   - How do you play your new game?

Tip

Don't try to change too much. Just change one or two things that will make the game more fun to play.

B ★ 📝 **Practise saying your instructions for your new game aloud. Use your notes to help you while you speak. Try teaching your game to some friends.**

1 Look at your notes again. Is there anything you need to remember to do? Write it on your notes.

2 How could you improve your instructions? Write any new ideas on your notes.

11 Write instructions

A 📝 **AZ** **Write your instructions for playing the party game you invented in the last session.**

Tip

As you write, think about your readers.

- Are you giving them enough information?
- Are the instructions in the right order?
- Do the instructions begin with a sequencing word or a command verb?

12 Improve your instructions

A 📖 Re-read your instructions.

1 Have you followed your notes and written the steps in the right order? Do you need to add any sequencing words?

2 Have you used command verbs and the present tense all the way through?

B 📝 **AZ** Are there any mistakes in your writing? Check it carefully.

- Have you used full stops and capital letters?
- Are there any missing words? (It's easy to miss out little words.)
- Is your spelling correct? Use a dictionary to check.
- Rewrite any words or sentences that are hard to read. Make sure your handwriting is clear.

> Now you're ready to have your party! Enjoy playing your game and have lots of fun!

How did I do?

C 💬 In this unit you have read instructions for making:

- a cake
- a pop-up card
- some fruit rockets.

Talk about what was the same about all of the texts and what was different. What did you learn about instructions? Which other text types do you remember from this unit?

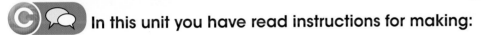

invitations   information   lists   letters   real-life stories

D 📝 You have learned about verbs. Are these sentences true? Copy the true sentences into your notebook.

1 Verbs are naming words: they tell you what things are called.

2 Verbs tell you what someone or something is, has or does.

3 Verbs are describing words.

4 Verbs tell you when an action happens: they tell you the tense.

E 📝 You have learned about suffixes. **Look at the instructions then copy and fill in the table in your notebook.**

Use the suffix **tion** to turn a verb into a noun.

Add the suffix **y** to turn a noun into an adjective.

Add the suffix **ly** to turn an adjective into an adverb.

Word	Word with suffix
invite	invitation
quiet	quietly
celebrate	
nice	
rain	
sad	
decorate	

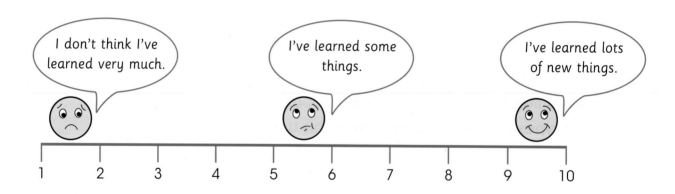

I don't think I've learned very much.

I've learned some things.

I've learned lots of new things.

1   2   3   4   5   6   7   8   9   10

3 See, hear, feel, enjoy

In this unit you will read and write some poems and short play scripts. The poems are all about one or more of the five senses – sight, hearing, smell, taste and touch.

You will also learn about:

nouns and noun phrases, adverbs, adjectives.

1 Breakfast

 A
 B
 C
 D
 E

A 💬 We find out about the world around us using our five senses. The five senses are sight, hearing, smell, taste and touch.

1 Look at the photos. Which senses are being used in each one?

2 Which sense do you think makes you happiest? Why?

Breakfast

Good morning little earthworm
  said the speckled thrush
Where would you be going
  so early in a rush
I'm off to find some breakfast
  he answered with a frown
Well so am I sir said the thrush
  and quickly gulped him down.

P.H. Kilby

How do you think the thrush and the earthworm might speak?

B 📖 ⭐ **AZ** Read *Breakfast* on page 37. Think about the sense of taste as you read the poem.

- When you have read the poem a couple of times to yourself, practise reading it aloud to a talk partner.
- When you have read it several times, try reading it aloud with expression. Can your talk partner understand it better?

C 📝 Answer these questions about the poem in your notebook.

1 There are two characters in the poem. Who or what are they?
2 What time of day is it?
3 Where does the earthworm say he is going?
4 Does he get there? Explain your answer.

Any volunteers
There isn't very much punctuation in the poem *Breakfast*. Copy the poem into your notebook, adding the punctuation. Does the punctuation help you to read aloud with expression?

2 Poem to play script

A 📖 ⭐ **AZ** Turn the poem *Breakfast* into a play.

1 Re-read the poem to yourself.
2 Now read it again in a group of three. One of you should read the thrush's lines, one the earthworm's lines and one will read all the other lines.
3 Look at the play script called *Breakfast*. Read it aloud several times in your group. Try to read it with expression.

In a play, the words that a character speaks are called his or her **lines**.

Breakfast

Early one morning in the garden
Thrush: Good morning, little earthworm.
  Where would you be going so
  early in a rush?
Earthworm: *(crossly)* I'm off to find some breakfast.
Thrush: Well, so am I, sir.
Thrush quickly gulps down Earthworm.

B 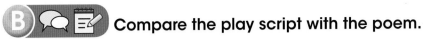 **Compare the play script with the poem.**

1 Discuss these questions:

   a How do you know who is talking in the play script?

   b Which bits do you read? How do you know?

   c Why are some bits of the play script written in brackets?

   d How many people do you need to read this play script?

   e Does the poem look the same as the play script on the page?

2 Copy the table into your notebook and fill it in with things that are the same about the play script and the poem, and things that are different.

Things that are the same	Things that are different

Language focus

Adverbs give you more information about a verb. In play scripts, adverbs are sometimes used to tell a character how to speak. Can you find an example in the *Breakfast* play script?

3 Write a play script

A 📖 ⭐ **Read the short poem about a hummingbird. Then read it aloud with expression to a talk partner.**

Did you know?

The word *dumb* has more than one meaning. It means someone who can't speak and it is also a rude word for someone you think is being silly or not very clever.

Hummingbird

Hummingbird, hummingbird, why
  don't you hum?
I do not hum because I am dumb.
  Then why are you called humming
bird of all things?
  Because of the noise that I make
with my wings.

                Odette Thomas

B ✍ **AZ** **Answer these questions in your notebook.**

1 Look at this list. Copy the two things that are true about the poem.
   a The poem tells us where hummingbirds live.
   b The poem tells us about the hummingbird's song.
   c The poem tells us how big hummingbirds are.
   d The poem tells us why hummingbirds are called hummingbirds.
   e The poem tells us what hummingbirds look like.

2 Which senses does the poem talk about – sight, hearing, smell, taste or touch?

3 Find two pairs of rhyming words in the poem and write them in your notebook.

4 Who is *I* in the poem?

C ✍ ⭐ **Turn the poem into a play script.**

1 Write the poem *Hummingbird* as a short play script in your notebook. Look at the layout of the play script on page 38 to help you. Invent a setting (some information about **where** the dialogue takes place) and a character (**who** is talking to the hummingbird). Include at least one adverb, telling the speaker how to say the line.

2 Perform the play script. Think about how to make the characters sound interesting when you perform your play.

4 Poems and the senses

Snail

Steady explorer
you crawl on your stomach foot
along silver trails;
stretch your soft neck, grasp a leaf
rasp it with sandpaper tongue.

Patricia Leighton

A 📖 📝 **AZ** Read the poem *Snail* and think about which senses it talks about. Then answer these questions in your notebook.

1 The poem's title is *Snail* but the word *snail* is not in the poem. Which words does the poet use instead?

2 What colour is the snail's trail?

3 List three of a snail's body parts that are mentioned in the text.

4 Which of the senses does the poem talk about – sight, hearing, smell, taste or touch?

Tip

Sometimes there will be a word that you don't know. For example, do you know what the word *rasp* in the last line means? If you don't know what a word means, would you:

• ignore it?

• pretend you know what it means?

• look it up in a dictionary?

• work out its meaning from other words nearby?

What do you think is the best thing to do? Why?

B 💬 The poet uses language that is precise and accurate to make a good picture in the reader's mind.

1 Why do you think the poet chose the word *crawl* instead of *go*?

2 Why did she use *rasp* instead of *eat*?

3 What information does *sandpaper* give you about the snail's tongue?

A snail's tongue

Did you know?

A snail's tongue is called a *radula*. It is covered in teeth. The radula works like a file, shredding food into tiny pieces.

C 💬 ⭐ Find more poems about the senses.

1 Talk about the meanings of any unfamiliar words.

2 Practise reading the poems aloud in class.

5 Write a poem

1

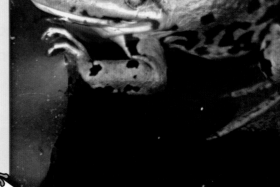

Frog

Water animal
you swim
in a pond.
You sit still and catch flies
with your tongue.

2

Frog

Hopping pond-dweller
swim with webbed feet
across the pond's scummy surface;
sit statue-still. Snatch a fly
with a quick flick of your sticky-tape tongue.

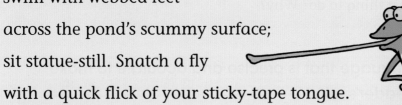

 **Read and discuss both *Frog* poems above.**

- How are these poems similar to the *Snail* poem on page 40?
- Which *Frog* poem do you prefer? Why?
- Which of the senses does the second *Frog* poem talk about – sight, hearing, smell, taste or touch?

I'm not just a duck – I'm a small, happy duck!

Language focus

Nouns are naming words. The words *elephant, phone* and *toothbrush* are nouns.

Adjectives are describing words which tell you more about a noun. The words *big, grey, shiny* and *bristly* are all adjectives.

A **noun phrase** is a group of words which takes the place of a noun. *The big grey elephant, a shiny phone* and *some bristly toothbrushes* are all noun phrases.

B **Look at the Language focus box about nouns and noun phrases.**

1 The table below has a list of some nouns and noun phrases in poem 1. Look at the list and find the words in the first poem.

2 Now look at poem 2. Which noun or noun phrase in the second poem does the same job as each of the nouns or noun phrases in the first poem? What is different?

3 Copy the table into your notebook and fill it in with the nouns and noun phrases from poem 2.

Nouns and noun phrases	
Poem 1	Poem 2
water animal	
a pond	
flies	
your tongue	

C **Write your own poem about an animal. Base your poem on *Snail*.**

Tip

Think of an animal you have seen and which you can describe. Use:

• interesting noun phrases which will tell the reader more about the animal

• good verbs which really describe how the animal moves

• words to make the reader think about what the animal looks, feels, sounds or smells like

• words which give descriptions of what the animal is and does.

6 Publish your poem

Language focus

Adverbs make **verbs** more precise or more interesting. For example, compare *It sits* with *It sits still*: *sits* is a verb but *sits still* is a verb with an adverb, telling you *how* it sits. Alternatively you might want to use the powerful verb *crouches* instead of *sits*.

Adjectives make **nouns** more interesting. For example, compare *surface* with **scummy** *surface*: *surface* is a noun but *scummy surface* is a noun with an adjective and is more descriptive.

A 📖 📝 **AZ** Look at the **Language focus** box. Then re-read the poem you wrote in the last session.

1 Improve three words by choosing a more descriptive word instead, or by adding an adjective or adverb to them.

2 Check the spelling of the three words.
Use a dictionary or check them on the internet.

Tip

You need to know the alphabet to use a dictionary. Check you know it!

A B C D E F G H I J K L M N
O P Q R S T U V W X Y Z

B 📝 Publish your poem. Write your poem out in your best handwriting or produce a final version on a computer. Add a picture of your animal.

How did I do?

C 💬 📝 In this unit you have read and written short play scripts and poems.

1 Discuss these questions without looking back at page 38.
- What is special about the layout of a play script?
- Do you use speech marks in play scripts?
- Why do you write some words and sentences in brackets?
- Why are adverbs important in play scripts?

Now turn back to page 38 and see how much you remembered.

2 The poems about snails and frogs didn't rhyme. How did you know you were reading a poem not a description in a non-fiction book?

3 All the poems in this unit talked about using one or more of the senses. Why do you think the poet wanted to make you think of different senses?

4 Write these descriptions in your notebook. Then write next to each one the sense that it refers to.

> moonlight-silver trail   rough, rasping tongue   piercing scream
> deliciously mouth-watering   the odour of decay

 hearing?    taste?   sight?   smell?   touch?

D 📝 **Adverbs tell us how, where or when an action happened. Find the adverb in each of these sentences.**

1 The cat ran quickly over the road.

2 It sat still and watched a bird.

3 Eventually the bird moved.

4 The cat looked around.

5 The cat got up very slowly.

6 Suddenly, it pounced.

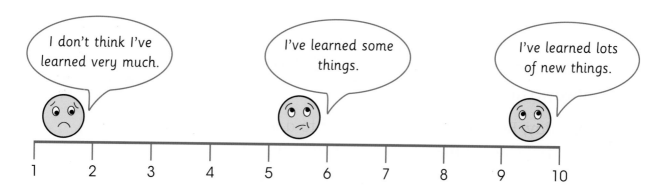

I don't think I've learned very much.

I've learned some things.

I've learned lots of new things.

1 2 3 4 5 6 7 8 9 10

4 Fiery beginnings

In this unit you will find out about myths, legends and fables. All the stories in the unit are about fire. At the end of the unit you will write your own fable.

You will also learn about: pronouns, paragraphs and adverbs, simple and compound sentences.

1 A roaring fire

A ⬤ AZ What do you know about fire?

- Is it useful? What for?
- Is it dangerous? How?
- What does it look like? Is it colourful?
- How does fire move? How does it sound?
- Which words can you use to talk about fire?

> wandered   glowing   dwindled   burned   blazing   roared
> delicious   flickering   smoke   flame   forest   wood

Bear and Fire

1. In the beginning, Bear owned Fire. Fire warmed Bear and his people on cold days and it gave them light when the nights were long and dark. Bear always carried Fire with him.

2. One day, Bear and his people went to a forest. Bear put Fire down at the edge of the forest, then Bear and his people went deeper and deeper into the forest to look for food.

3. Fire blazed up happily for a while until it had burned nearly all of its wood. It started to smoke and flicker, then it dwindled down and down. Fire was worried. It was nearly out. "Feed me! Feed me!"

shouted Fire. But Bear and his people had wandered deep into the forest, and they did not hear Fire's cries.

4 At that moment, Man came walking through the forest and saw the small, flickering Fire. "Feed me! Feed me!" cried Fire.

"What should I feed you?" Man asked. He had never seen Fire before.

"I eat sticks and logs," Fire replied.

Man picked up a stick and gave it to Fire. Fire sent its flames flickering up the side of the stick until the stick started to burn. Man brought more and more sticks and Fire leapt and danced in delight.

5 Man warmed himself by the blazing Fire, enjoying the colours of the flames and the hissing sound Fire made as it ate the wood. Man and Fire were very happy together and Man fed Fire sticks whenever it got hungry.

6 A long time later, Bear and his people came back to the edge of the forest, looking for Fire. Fire was angry when it saw Bear and it jumped and roared at him and drove him away.

7 So from that day to this, Fire has belonged to Man.

B 📖 💬 Many stories from around the world explain how people discovered fire. *Bear and Fire* comes from the Alabama Tribe of Native Americans. Storytelling is still very important to them because they learn about their culture and history through stories.

1 Read *Bear and Fire*.
2 What do you think of the story?
   Are there any questions you would like to ask about it?

C  **Answer these questions in your notebook.**

1 How was Fire useful to Bear and his people?
2 Why didn't Bear take Fire into the forest with him?
3 How did Man know what to feed Fire?
4 What did Man like about Fire?
5 Why do you think Fire wouldn't go back to Bear?

2 Myths

A **AZ** Myths are a special kind of traditional tale. First look at the **Language focus** box about myths. Then re-read *Bear and Fire* and talk about the story.

1 Why is there only one Bear, one Man and one Fire?
2 The story begins with the words *In the beginning*. When do you think that was?
3 Do you think this is a true story? Why or why not?
4 Can you find any of the features of myths in *Bear and Fire*? Which ones?

Language focus

A myth is a traditional story, sometimes thousands of years old. Myths were passed on from person to person by word of mouth. Myths often contain:

● characters named after an animal or something from the natural world
● information which explains *why* or *how* something is
● characters that are not of this world, such as gods and goddesses
● things that don't happen in the real world.

B ★ **Talk about the character Fire.**

1 What do you know about Fire from the story?
2 Discuss these words and choose the three that best describe Fire.

> proud friendly timid playful exciting
> happy gloomy grateful angry

3 Perform the story in groups. First decide who is going to play each of the characters. Then act out the story.

3 Pronouns

A **AZ** Look at the **Language focus** box. Copy these sentences into your notebook. Underline the pronoun or pronouns in each one.

1 Fire warmed Bear and his people and it also gave them light.
2 Bear put Fire down and left it behind while he went to look for food.
3 When it had burned up all of its wood, Fire started to call for help.
4 Man heard it. He came to help and he fed it sticks.

Is your handwriting joined up? Are you leaving the right amount of space between your letters and your words? Do your letters **b**, **d**, **f**, **h**, **k**, **l** and **t** stick up higher? Do **f**, **g**, **j**, **p**, **q**, and **y** hang below the line?

Language focus

Pronouns can be used instead of nouns or noun phrases.

The words *Bear*, *Fire*, *forest* and *stick* are all nouns.

Bear and his people and *small, flickering fire* are both noun phrases.

The words *he, she, it, you, him, they* and *them* are all pronouns.

B Re-read *Bear and Fire*. How many different pronouns can you find in the story? Make a list of pronouns in your notebook.

How to write a legend

You will need:
- a hero or heroine as the main character
- a dangerous task (sometimes involving a monster or a powerful enemy)
- an event in the past that is true or was possibly true, or an event linked to a culture or a set of beliefs

What to do:
1 Explain when in history the legend is set.
2 Introduce the main character.
3 Explain how difficult and dangerous the task is.
4 Make the main character very brave.
5 Make sure the main character is successful.

There are stories of the Queen of Sheba in many of the world's religions.

A ★ 💬 **AZ** Read the recipe for legends. Talk about the differences between legends and myths. Do you know any legends from your history or culture? Are there stories about famous heroes or heroines who lived in your part of the world?

King Solomon and the Queen of Sheba

1 Over 3500 years ago, the Queen of Sheba began to hear strange tales. The traders who came to her African kingdom told tales of a new king. "King Solomon," they said, "is a very wise man." The queen asked questions about this new king. She watched the traders' faces in the flickering light of the fires and saw that in the stories they told her about the king, they spoke the truth. "There are already legends about this man," she said to her closest advisers. "I must meet him so I can decide for myself how wise he is." She ordered her servants to prepare a train of camels and load them with gifts for the king.

2 After a few weeks, the queen was ready to set out. Throughout the long journey she rode her own camel. She sat on a silken cushion and was protected from the harsh sunlight by a silken canopy over her head. The journey across the desert was dangerous so many died from thirst or exhaustion. There were also fierce fights with bandits who wanted to steal the camels.

3 When King Solomon knew that the queen was coming, he told his servants to polish the floor of his throne room floor until it was as shiny as a mirror and to set many lamps to blaze around the walls. The light from the torches reflected in the mirror-like floor so the room was bathed in dancing flames. King Solomon had heard a strange story about the queen. It was said that the beautiful queen had one leg that was hairy like a goat's and Solomon wanted to know if this was true.

4 At long last, the queen's train of camels approached the palace. The king sent torch-bearers out into the desert to meet her so she came to his city in a glittering procession of torchlight. As he led the queen into his court, Solomon glanced down at the floor. It was true! She did have a hairy leg!

5 Soon the queen's leg was forgotten. King Solomon and the Queen of Sheba became good friends and the queen stayed at King Solomon's court for many months.

Did you know?

Torches were made from bunches of reeds which were soaked in animal fat. This made a light that would burn slowly.

B 📖 📝 Read the legend *King Solomon and the Queen of Sheba*. Which features of legends can you find in the story? Now answer these questions about the story in your notebook.

1 Who told the queen of King Solomon's wisdom?
2 Why was the journey dangerous?
3 What was odd about the queen?
4 Why did Solomon tell his servants to polish the floor?

Why do you think there is an exclamation mark after *She did have a hairy leg!* in the story? How will you read these words?

5 Paragraphs

A 📖 📝 **AZ** A paragraph is a section of a text.

1 First divide a large piece of paper into six boxes.
2 Then re-read the story *King Solomon and the Queen of Sheba*.
   • Decide which you think are the five most important events in the story.
   • In five of the boxes, draw a picture to show the events in the right order.
   • Re-read the story. Have you drawn one picture for each of the paragraphs?
   • If you have time, write words or phrases from the story about fire in the sixth box.

Tip

Plan what you will draw in each of the boxes **before** you begin to draw it.

B 📝 Look at the numbered paragraphs in the story again. Find the first word or phrase (a group of words) in each paragraph. What information do they give? Write the words or phrases in your notebook.

Language focus

Adverbs tell you how, where and when events take place. Words such as *when*, *soon* and *after* are adverbs.

Phrases, or groups of words, such as *At long last* and *Over 3500 years ago* are adverbial phrases, or adverbials, which act like adverbs.

Language focus

A **simple sentence** has only one verb or verb phrase. For example:

At long last, the queen's train of camels **approached** the palace.

Solomon **had heard** a strange story about the queen. It **was** true!

Simple sentences can be joined together using joining words to make compound sentences.

A **compound sentence** is made up of two simple sentences joined with *and*, *but*, *so* or *or*. For example:

"I **must** meet him **so** I **can decide** for myself how wise he is."

(Sentence 1 = "I **must** meet him.")

Sentence 2 = "I **can decide** for myself how wise he is.")

A 📝 **AZ** Can you find the verb in each of these simple sentences? (There are two sentences in each line.) List the verbs in your notebook.

1   The traders knew stories about King Solomon. The queen talked to the traders.
2   The queen went to visit King Solomon. She took gifts with her.
3   The journey was dangerous. The queen went anyway.
4   The king prepared his palace. There were torches on the walls.
5   The queen arrived. King Solomon invited her in.
6   Solomon looked at the mirror-like floor. He saw the queen's leg.

B 📝 Join the pairs of simple sentences in Activity A together using *and*, *but*, *so* or *or* to make compound sentences. Write the six compound sentences in your notebook.

Tip

You can use pronouns in some of your compound sentences. Which pronoun will you use instead of *the traders*?

The traders knew stories about King Solomon so the queen talked to the traders.

C 📖 💬 Work with a partner to find more compound sentences that are used in the story.

See if you can find five compound sentences and write them in your notebook. Underline the verbs in each sentence and talk about how the sentences are joined.

Language focus

Sometimes nouns and pronouns are missed out in compound sentences. For example, you can write:

- either: **She** sat on a silken cushion and **she** was protected from the harsh sunlight by a silken canopy over her head.
- or: **She** sat on a silken cushion and was protected from the harsh sunlight by a silken canopy over her head.

7 Fables

A 📖 📝 **AZ** Read *The Monkey and the Cat*, a fable by Aesop. Then answer these questions in your notebook.

1 How many characters lived in the house?
2 Why didn't the monkey want to get the chestnuts out of the fire?
3 How did the monkey persuade the cat to get them for him?
4 What is your opinion of the cat?

Language focus

This story is a fable. **Fables** are short stories that are usually about talking animals. The animals in fables usually each have a particular characteristic and behave in a particular way. So, for example:

- foxes are cunning – they play tricks on the other animals
- owls are wise – they are clever and give good advice
- dogs are foolish but loyal – they do silly things but they are good animals
- horses and elephants are strong.

The purpose of a fable is to teach a lesson about something. Sometimes the writer tells you very clearly what the idea is that he or she wants you to learn; sometimes you have to work it out from what happens in the story. This lesson is called the **moral** of the story.

The Monkey and the Cat

1 A monkey and a cat once lived together with an old man. They were good friends.

2 One evening they were warming themselves by the fire. They could smell the delicious smell of the chestnuts that were roasting in the flames.

3 At last the monkey became so hungry that he tried to pick a chestnut out of the fire. "Ow!" he complained. "That's too hot! I can't get it!"

4 Then he looked slyly at the cat and said, "I have a plan. You are so much braver than me. A bit of pain won't worry you. If you put your paw into the fire and pull out the chestnuts, we can share them."
The cat liked the monkey so she put her paw into the fire, just as her friend had asked her to do.

5 The cat began pulling the chestnuts out of the fire. But as fast as she pulled them out, the monkey grabbed them and gobbled them up.

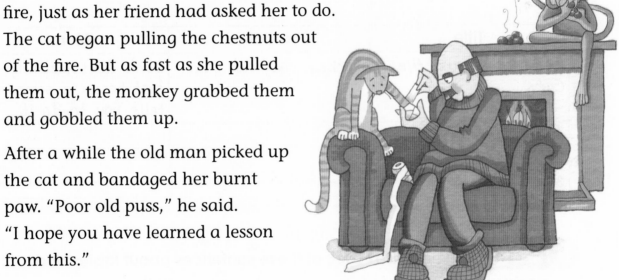

6 After a while the old man picked up the cat and bandaged her burnt paw. "Poor old puss," he said. "I hope you have learned a lesson from this."

Did you know?

Aesop was a slave in ancient Greece who wrote many fables. Much later, in the 17th century, a Frenchman called Jean de la Fontaine rewrote some of Aesop's fables. People still read the stories today.

The word *cat's-paw* is sometimes used to mean someone who is used by other people to do things that they don't want to do themselves.

B 💬 📝 Re-read the story. Then re-read the **Language focus** box about fables on page 55. Discuss the following questions:

1 How do you know *The Monkey and the Cat* is a fable?

2 In fables, foxes are clever and owls are wise. What do you think monkeys are in fables? And what about cats?

3 What is the lesson – or moral – of this fable?

8 More about fables

A 📖 📝 **AZ** Read and discuss three more fables. Try looking on the internet or in the library.

1 Think about the characters and the lesson in the fables. Is the moral clear?

2 Copy the table into your notebook and fill it in for the fables you read.

Title	Characters	Moral
The Monkey and the Cat	monkey, cat, old man	Don't do something just because someone tells you to do it.
1		
2		
3		

B 📖 📝 True or false? Look at these sentences about fables and decide which ones are true and which are false. Write the true sentences in your notebook.

1 The setting is described with lots of adjectives (describing words).

2 It's told in the past tense.

3 The characters are described with lots of adjectives.

4 It's short.

5 There's only one main event.

6 The main characters are often talking animals.

7 There's always a clear lesson or moral.

8 One of the characters 'wins'.

9 There are lots of characters.

Language focus

In *The Monkey and the Cat*, we know that the monkey is male because the pronoun *he* is sometimes used instead of the noun *monkey*.

We also know that the cat is female because the pronoun *she* is used instead of the noun *cat*.

The pronouns **he**, **him** and **himself**, and the possessive adjective **his** (as in ***his*** plan), show that a character is **male**.

The pronouns **she**, **her** and **herself**, and the possessive adjective **her** (as in ***her*** paw), show that a character is **female**.

9 Making links

A Look back over the previous sessions on myths, legends and fables. What have you learned about the features of each type of text? Are there any features which link the different text types? Remind yourself of the features of each and talk about what is the same and what is different. Record your ideas on a class 'Features' chart.

B Compare and contrast the three stories in this unit.

1 Re-read the myth *Bear and Fire* on page 46.
2 Then re-read the legend *King Solomon and the Queen of Sheba* on page 50.
3 Finally re-read the fable *The Monkey and the Cat* on page 54.
4 Now copy this table into your notebook. Decide what is the same about the stories and what is different. Fill in the table.

	Myth *Bear and Fire*	Legend *King Solomon and the Queen of Sheba*	Fable *The Monkey and the Cat*
When?			
Where?			
Characters			
Main event			
Theme/lesson/ moral	How people got fire		

10 Plan a fable

A 📖 ⭐ The fable *The Monkey and the Cat* has three characters: the monkey, the cat and the old man. What would happen if you changed the characters? Would they behave in the same way?

1 Re-read the fable *The Monkey and the Cat*.
2 In groups, role play the story.
3 Decide on some different characters for the fable and explore what happens.
4 Decide on one story for your new fable.

> **Any volunteers?**
> If you had a fox and an elephant, how do you think the story would change?

B 💬 Make sure you understand how the fable works. Look at the paragraphs in the fable:

- Paragraph 1 introduces the characters.
- Paragraph 2 introduces the setting.
- Paragraph 3 main event 1 – one character wants something he can't get.
- Paragraph 4 main event 2 – he persuades the other character to get it for him.
- Paragraph 5 main event 3 – the other character gets the object.
- Paragraph 6 ends the fable and gives the moral.

C 📝 ⭐ Make a storyboard.

1 Divide a piece of paper into four boxes.
2 In boxes 1–3, draw the main events of your fable.
3 In box 4, collect some words you could use when you write your fable. You could borrow some words from the stories in this unit for your word bank, or you could use some of the phrases from other fables you have read.

> A storyboard is a plan. Cartoons and other films are always planned as a series of pictures on a storyboard.

Tip

Remember to include some adverbs and adverbial phrases in your word bank. They are the words to tell you when, where or how something happened. You can use them at the start of your paragraphs.

11 Write a fable

(A) 📝 ⭐ **Look again at the storyboard you made in the last session.**

1 Practise telling yourself your fable. Use the words and phrases (including the adverbs) from your word bank. Are you happy with the story for your fable? Do you need to make any changes to it?

2 Practise telling your story to a talk partner. Has your partner got any suggestions for your story?

(B) 📝 **AZ** Write your story. Try to include some dialogue. Use the **Language focus** box to help you. When you have finished writing it, read your story aloud to check it. Add in any little words you might have missed out. Correct any mistakes in your writing.

> ## Language focus
>
> **Dialogue** is another term for speech in stories. When you write dialogue you:
> - start a new speaker on a new line
> - use speech marks around the words characters say.
>
> Speech marks like this " show where the words a character says **begin**.
> Speech marks like this " show where the words a character says **end**.
> Phrases like *he said* are not included inside the speech marks. For example:
> *"Use speech marks like this," he said.*
> There are lots of different words you can use instead of *said* like *asked, replied, shouted, muttered.*

12 Improve your fable

(A) 📝 Re-read your writing from the previous session.
Find at least three things to improve in your writing.

- Does your fable make sense? Have you missed out any important ideas?
- Check your opening and ending. Are they right for this story?
- Check the vocabulary. Can you use more powerful or more descriptive words.
- Check your sentences. Have you used some good joining words?
- Check you haven't made any mistakes with your punctuation and spelling.

(B) 📝 **AZ** **What have you done well? What could you do better next time?**

- Write two statements about what you are pleased with in your story.
- Write one target for something you want to improve on.

How did I do?

C 📝 In this unit you have read a myth, a legend and some fables. You also learned about:

- pronouns
- compound sentences
- paragraphs and adverbial phrases.

1 Copy the table about myths, legends and fables into your notebook.

2 Read the statements and tick which type of story they are true for. Some are true for more than one.

	Myths	Legends	Fables
The stories were told before they were written down.	✓	✓	✓
The stories are set in the past.			
The stories explain how or why something happens.			
The stories are about heroes and gods.			
The characters are usually animals.			
There is usually a lesson or moral.			

D 📝 Make these pairs of sentences into compound sentences by joining them with *and, but, so* or *or*. Replace some of the nouns and noun phrases with pronouns.

1 The elephant lived in the jungle. The elephant was allergic to trees.

2 The cow was feeling hungry. The cow ate all the flowers in the park.

3 Does Stefan like cats? Does Stefan prefer dogs?

4 The teacher looked at the children. The children stopped talking.

5 The giant looked down at the people. The giant laughed.

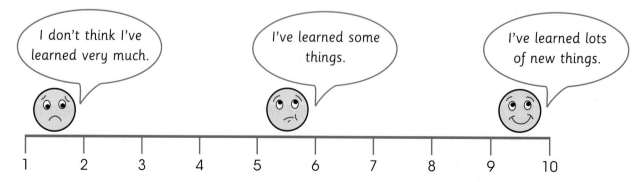

I don't think I've learned very much.

I've learned some things.

I've learned lots of new things.

1   2   3   4   5   6   7   8   9   10

5 Letters

This unit is about letters. In the unit you will read various letters and postcards, written for different reasons and to different people. You will plan and write letters of your own.

You will also learn about: synonyms, apostrophes, singular and plural nouns, sentence punctuation.

1 Letters and postcards

A 💬 When do you and your friends send or receive mail? When do your parents and other adults send or receive it?

B 📖 💬 **AZ** Why do we write letters?
1 Read the three texts. What sort of text are they?
2 Why do you think each of the texts was written? How do you know?

1

Dear Aunty Sonia,

Thank you for the books you kindly gave me for my birthday. I was too excited after my party to read, but I intend to start a book immediately after I have finished this letter.

How did you know that Francesca Simon was my favourite fiction writer? I love reading about her characters and their adventures. They make me laugh so hard. Do you think I'm more like Horrid Henry or Perfect Peter?

I know you know how interested I am in cars and the non-fiction book about cars is amazing. I really like the section on huge, powerful cars! One of my ambitions is to drive a car of this sort when I grow up.

Lots of love

Arturo

2

The Manager

Correo Argentino

Dear Sir

Re: Late delivery of letters

I am writing to complain about the fact that some letters that were posted in your area took over five weeks to reach me. A number of letters were written and posted on the same day. The first arrived within ten days of being posted, but the last of these letters took nearly four times as long.

These letters were very important to me for they were written by people I care about. I am away from my home at the moment so it is particularly important to me that I receive letters promptly.

I would be grateful for an explanation as to why some of these letters took so long.

Yours faithfully

Mrs S. Sabella

3

Dear Class 3,

Look at what I saw in England today! The sound of all those feet marching and stamping at the same time was so loud! Even louder than the trumpets! I love all those red uniforms and funny, fluffy hats. Luckily the sun shone for us. I'll have so much to tell you when I get back to Argentina.

From Mrs Sabella

Did you know?

Every country has its own stamps. You can tell where a letter comes from by the stamp on the envelope. Where do these stamps come from?

2 Scanning or reading carefully?

A You can read in different ways. You can scan a text quickly when you want to find a particular word or piece of information. You can read a text slowly and carefully when you need to make sure you understand it completely. Scan the text to answer these three questions. Write the answers in your notebook.

1 Who wrote the text?
2 Where is she going?
3 Why is she going away?

Dear Class 3,

Yesterday, I had some very sad news. My mother, who lives in London, is very ill. I have to go to England to see her. When I am there, I will stay with my sister and her family. The good thing for me is that I will get to see my nephew, Arturo, who is the same age as you.

The other bad news is that I may be away from Argentina for a few weeks. While I am away, Mrs Diaz will be your teacher. Please work hard for her and show her what wonderful children you are and how much you have learned so far this year.

I will write to you from England and tell you what I am doing. I hope you will write to me too. I will miss you all.

From Mrs Sabella

B 📖 📝 **AZ** Now read the text slowly and carefully to find the answers to these questions. Write the answers in your notebook.

1 Who is Arturo?

2 Does the writer like Class 3?

C 💬 Share your answers to Activities A and B with a talk partner. Talk about the difference between scanning and reading carefully.

3 A good day out

Dear Class 3,

Yesterday, my sister looked after my mother for the day so Arturo and I went for a day out in London. We had a very enjoyable time.

First we went to see Buckingham Palace, where Queen Elizabeth lives. It's a huge house. Arturo and I counted 68 windows! Why do you imagine the Queen and her husband need that many rooms?

After leaving the palace, we strolled in the sun beside the river Thames. It's a very wide river, and it's extremely busy with ships, speedboats, water taxis and water buses. There are even river police!

Then we went to Westminster and saw the Houses of Parliament. This is where the government makes the laws in the UK. The Houses of Parliament are next to the Thames.

Finally we went across Westminster Bridge for a ride on the London Eye. This was Arturo's favourite part of the day! The London Eye is a massive wheel. You've probably seen it on TV because they set off fireworks from the London Eye for important celebrations. You can see some excellent views of London from the top.

I hope you are working hard and learning lots of things. I miss you all.

From Mrs Sabella

 **Read Mrs Sabella's letter from London. Talk about these questions.**

Does she say:

- what happened?
- who was there?
- when it happened?
- where it happened?
- why or how it happened?

Tip

Decide whether you need to scan the letter or read it carefully to answer each question.

B **AZ** **Answer these questions in your notebook.**

1 List three things that Mrs Sabella and Arturo saw.
2 What did Mrs Sabella find surprising about Buckingham Palace?
3 When is the London Eye on TV?

C **Mrs Sabella used some interesting words in her letter. Can you find some of the interesting words she used? Why do you think she used them?**

1 Copy the table into your notebook.
2 Beside each word, write a word or words from the box that have the same meaning.

> enjoyable   excellent   house   huge   imagine   massive
> palace   ship   speedboat   strolled   water taxi   wide

Ordinary word	Synonyms
big	
nice	
walked	
building	
boat	
think	

London looks like an interesting place to visit. The river Thames sounds busy – or I could say **hectic**!

Language focus

Synonyms are words that have similar meanings. For example, *cheerful* is a synonym of *happy*; *miserable* is a synonym of *sad*.

Using synonyms of ordinary words can make your writing more interesting and precise, and this helps the reader to understand what you want to say better.

4 An interesting experience

A 📝💬 **What have you seen or done recently that was interesting? Decide on an event you can talk about.**

1 Make a plan in your notebook. Jot down some things you would like to say in your talk. Remember to say:
   - what happened
   - who was there
   - when it happened
   - where it happened
   - why or how it happened.

2 Use your plan to tell your talk partner about your experience. Then give your talk to the class.

B 📝 **AZ** **Write a letter in reply to Mrs Sabella, telling her about the event you talked about in Activity A.**

Remember to use interesting words!

Language focus

An **apostrophe** shows where two words have been joined together and then shortened. For example, look at these words with apostrophes:

> I am → I'm   we are → we're   they will → they'll
> can not → can't   could not → couldn't

Can you see how the apostrophe replaces the missing letters?

5 Arturo's birthday

A 📖 📝 **Read Mrs Sabella's latest letter. What has been happening in England? Answer these questions in your notebook. Decide whether you need to scan for information or to read carefully.**

1 What sort of letter did Arturo send to his aunt, Mrs Sabella?
2 Where was Arturo's birthday party held?
3 What happened at the party?

Arturo

would like to invite
Aunty Sonia
to my 8th birthday party
on 24th May
from 4:30 to 6:00
at the Village Hall
RSVP

Dear Class 3,

Can you guess what's happening here?

Here's my party invitation from Arturo.

The party was very exciting. A cowboy came and showed us how to do tricks with a lasso. It was more difficult than it looked! Arturo thought it was wonderful.

I'll write a proper letter soon.

From

Mrs Sabella

Did you know?

Cowboys have different names in different parts of the word.
In Argentina they're called *gauchos*, in Australia they're *drovers*,
in California they're *buckaroos* and in Hungary they're *gulyás*.

Language focus

Most nouns have **singular** and **plural** forms. The word *singular* means one single thing. The word *plural* means more than one thing. For example, *book* is a singular noun, but *books* is a plural noun.

For most regular nouns, the plural form is made by adding **s**, **es** or **ies**.

Some irregular nouns have different plural forms.

B  **AZ** Look at the **Language focus** box on page 67.

1 Copy and fill in this table in your notebook.

Singular	Plural
birthday	birthdays
cowboy	
balloon	
cake	

2 What happens when a singular noun ends in a **consonant** + **y**? Copy and fill in this table in your notebook.

Singular	Plural
party	parties
story	
berry	
family	

3 What happens when a singular noun ends in **x**, **sh**, **s** or **ch**? Now copy and fill in this table in your notebook.

Singular	Plural
box	boxes
class	
brush	
bench	

4 Some nouns have **irregular plural forms**. Copy this table in your notebook. Fill it in with the plural nouns from the box.

people   sheep   feet   geese
men   children   mice   teeth

Singular	Plural
knife	knives
child	
mouse	
person	
tooth	
sheep	
goose	
foot	
man	

6 A letter of complaint

A 💬 **AZ** Look again at the letters on pages 61 and 62.

1 Which one of them is a letter of complaint? How do you know?

2 How is the letter of complaint different from Mrs Sabella's other letters in this unit? How is it the same?

B 📝 Can you find any compound sentences in Mrs Sabella's letter of complaint? Which joining words did she use?

Join these pairs of sentences using *and, but, so* or *or*.

Write the compound sentence in your notebook.

Any volunteers?
For help, look back at the
Language focus box on
page 53 in Unit 4.

1 Mrs Sabella will buy Arturo a birthday present. She will go to his party.
2 Mrs Sabella likes Arturo. She does not like his dog.
3 Mrs Sabella might buy Arturo a book. She might buy him a toy.
4 Arturo likes books. Mrs Sabella might buy him a book.
5 Mrs Sabella is Arturo's aunt. She loves him very much.

7 More about apostrophes

A 📖📝 **AZ** Read the letter from Mrs Sabella. Then answer the questions below in your notebook.

Dear Class 3,

It's been a long time since I last wrote to you because my mother was in hospital for a few weeks. She had an operation last week and now she's getting better. That's good news, isn't it? I have now left my sister's house and I am staying with my mother at her house. I will stay with my mother until she is completely better.

I was able to spend some time with Arturo last week. It was raining, so we had to stay inside. We spent an afternoon drawing pictures of things we have seen. I think Arturo's pictures were better than mine.

When I know that my mother is really better, I'll book my ticket back to Argentina. I hope you're all behaving well and working hard.

From Mrs Sabella

---

1 How many paragraphs are there in the letter?
2 Why has Mrs Sabella not written for a while?
3 Why do you think Mrs Sabella is not living with her sister and Arturo any more?
4 Why do you think Mrs Sabella wrote this letter?

Language focus

Apostrophes show where two words have been joined together and then shortened. They also show **possession** – when someone **has or owns** something.

Look at these words with apostrophes:

> Paula has got a book → Paula**'s** book
> Samir owns a coat → Samir**'s** coat
> the nephew of Mrs Sabella → Mrs Sabella**'s** nephew

Apostrophes show shortened words and they show possession.

Don't use an apostrophe to show plural nouns. For example, the plural of *ticket* is *tickets* – no apostrophe.

B Find the words with an apostrophe in Mrs Sabella's letter. In your notebook write a list of all the words with an apostrophe where the apostrophe shows words have been joined together and shortened.

Then write a list of all the words with an apostrophe to show possession.

8 Focus on writing

A Plan a reply to Mrs Sabella's letter of explanation in your notebook.

- What will you say about Mrs Sabella's letter?
- What will you tell Mrs Sabella?

Tip

When you reply to a letter, respond to some of the ideas in it.

B **AZ** Write your letter to Mrs Sabella. Remember to organise your ideas carefully in paragraphs.

Can you write quickly and neatly, with joined-up handwriting? Make sure your handwriting is neat. Are your letters the same size? Are **b**, **d**, **f**, **h**, **k**, **l** and **t** taller and do **f**, **g**, **j**, **p**, **q**, and **y** have tails below the line? Have you got even spaces between the letters and the words?

1

From: Sonia.Sabell7lemail.com

To: class 3.scolastmaria@baschools.arg

Subject: Leaving England

Dear Class 3,

I am coming back to Argentina. My mother is better now and she is able to be by herself. I have booked my ticket and I will leave tomorrow. The flight takes a long time, so I won't be home until Monday morning.

I will see you in school on Tuesday.

From Mrs Sabella

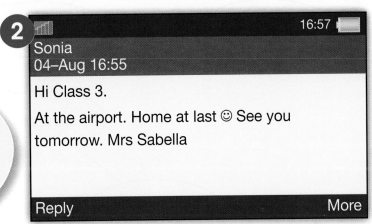

Remember that **verbs** tell you what someone or something does, is, or has. **Pronouns** are words like *it, I, she* and *mine*. They can replace nouns and noun phrases.

2

16:57

Sonia
04–Aug 16:55

Hi Class 3.

At the airport. Home at last ☺ See you tomorrow. Mrs Sabella

Reply   More

A 📖💬 **Read the two messages from Mrs Sabella. Did these messages come by post? How do you know?**

1 Are there any **verbs** in the email? What about in the SMS message?

2 Are there any **pronouns** in the email? What about in the SMS message?

3 Are there **sentences** in the email? What about in the SMS message?

B 📝 **AZ** **Change the SMS message into proper sentences. Write the message in sentences in your notebook.**

1 Underline the verbs in your sentences.

2 Circle the pronouns.

C 💬 **In groups, practise telling the story of Mrs Sabella's trip to England. Use the letters in this unit to help you.**

10 All sorts of mail

A 💬 **AZ** Talk about the different sorts of mail you receive at home.

1 Think of the different reasons people have for writing letters and emails.

2 Make a mind map on the board to show the different sorts of mail and the different reasons for writing them.

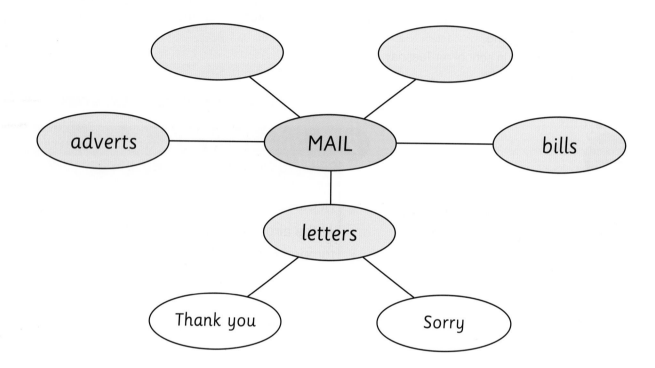

Did you know?

Every year the American mail service delivers about 212 billion pieces of mail – that's 212,000,000,000 items!

B 💬 Talk with a talk partner about a time when you got some mail. **(It can be fiction or a true story.)**

- Read the speech bubbles for the speaker and for the listener.
- Decide who will be the speaker and the listener.
- Speaker: practise telling your talk partner your mail story.
- Speaker and listener: tell each other whether you followed the tips in the speech bubbles.

Speaker

The way that you talk is as important as what you say.

Look at the people you are talking to.

Make your voice sound interesting.

Try to sound interested in what you are saying.

Listener

When you listen, the way you sit or stand can help the speaker.

Don't move around too much when you're listening to someone.

Look at the person who is talking to you.

Try to look interested in what the person is talking to you about.

11 Writing a letter

A Make a plan for a letter to Mrs Sabella, telling her about what you have been doing during the last month while she has been away in England. Make notes in your notebook to plan your ideas. Think about:

● how you can organise your ideas into paragraphs
● the vocabulary you will use, including powerful words to describe what you have done
● your sentences, including compound sentences using joining words.

B Write your letter to Mrs Sabella.

12 Improve your letter

(A) AZ Re-read your letter. Is your reason for writing clear? Can you:

- organise your ideas more clearly?
- join simple sentences into compound sentences using joining words?
- use more interesting vocabulary?

(B) Are there any mistakes in your writing? Check it carefully.

- Have you missed out any words?
- Have you used the past tense throughout?
- Look at the **Language focus** box. Is the punctuation correct?
- Are all words spelled correctly?
- Use a dictionary to check. Make a note of any words you found difficult to spell.

Language focus

Punctuation is important in your writing.

- Use a capital letter at the beginning of your sentences and for people's names and place names. End every sentence with a full stop (**.**), a question mark (**?**) or an exclamation mark (**!**).
- Use commas to separate items in lists.
- Use an apostrophe to show where you have joined two words together and shortened them, or to show possession.

How did I do?

(C) In this unit you have read a lot of letters which were written for different reasons. You have also learned more about:

- punctuation marks, including commas and apostrophes
- pronouns and compound sentences
- singular and plural nouns
- synonyms and choosing interesting words.

Talk about whether the following statements are true or false.

1 You usually write letters to people you like.
2 Letters are better than phone calls.
3 You should send a letter when you have information or ideas to share.
4 Letters can be about anything.
5 There is always a reason for writing a letter.
6 Letters always begin with the word *Dear.*

D 📝 **Copy these sentences into your notebook.**
Add the punctuation marks.

1 my name is carla and I am eight years old
2 did you hear what i said
3 you are my favourite friend
4 i dont know what to do so im going to cry

E 📝 **Find the synonyms. Match the words in the pink circle with the**
more interesting words in the blue circle. Then write the pairs of words
in your notebook.

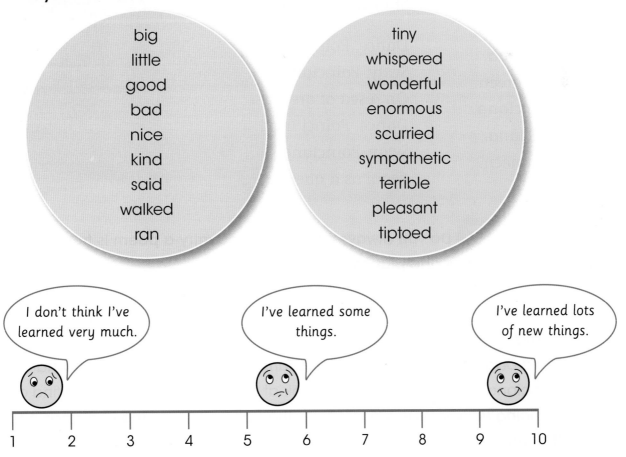

big	tiny
little	whispered
good	wonderful
bad	enormous
nice	scurried
kind	sympathetic
said	terrible
walked	pleasant
ran	tiptoed

I don't think I've learned very much.

I've learned some things.

I've learned lots of new things.

1 2 3 4 5 6 7 8 9 10

6 Poems from around the world

In this unit you will read and perform poems from around the world. You will think about how poems are linked to places, explore the words and sounds in the poems, and copy the style of some of the poems to write a poem of your own.

You will also learn about:
noun phrases, syllables.

1 Word pictures

Dancing Poinciana

Fire in the treetops,
Fire in the sky.
Blossoms red as sunset
Dazzling to the eye.

Dance, Poinciana,
Sway, Poinciana,
On a sea of green.
Dance, Poinciana,
Sway, Poinciana,
Regal as a queen.

Fire in the treetops,
Fire in the sky.
Crimson petals and white
Stained with scarlet dye.

Dance, Poinciana,
Sway, Poinciana,
On a sea of green.
Dance, Poinciana,
Sway, Poinciana,
Regal as a queen.

A 📖💬**AZ** Do you always know which country a poem is from? Talk about poems and places.

1 Talk about the clues there could be in a poem to tell you which country it was written in. If a poem was from your town, region or country, what would it say?

2 Read *Dancing Poinciana* by Telcine Turner. Can you guess who or what Poinciana is? (If you can't guess, look at the **Did you know**? box to find out.)

3 *Dancing Poinciana* is a poem from the Bahamas. Find the Bahamas on the map.

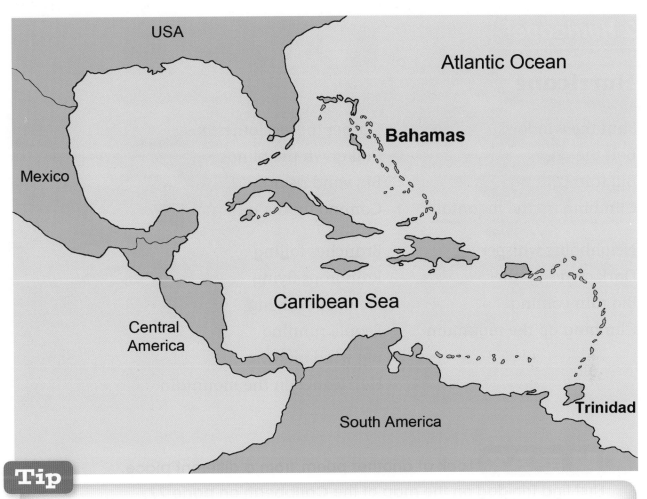

Remember, if you don't know what a word means, don't give up reading! Instead you can:

- think of another word that looks the same (e.g. *stained* looks like *stain*)
- read the rest of the sentence and see if you can work out the word
- look at the pictures – can you find information from them?
- ask someone or look the word up in a dictionary.

The Bahamas in the Atlantic Ocean, below the state of Florida, which is in the USA.

B Some of the words in *Dancing Poinciana* tell you about the Bahamas where the poem comes from. Others make pictures.

1 Which words in the poem tell you about the Bahamas?
2 Which words help you to see the tree inside your head?
3 What do you think of the poem? Can you tell where it comes from? Can you see the tree? Write about what the poem makes you think and see.

Did you know?

Poinciana is a tree with many names. Its scientific name is *Delonix regia*. but it is also known as a Royal Poinciana, Flame tree, or Gulmohar.

Hurricane

Shut the windows
Bolt the doors
Big rain coming
Climbing up the mountain

Neighbours whisper
Dark clouds gather
Big rain coming
Climbing up the mountain

Gather in the clothesline
Pull down the blinds
Big wind rising
Coming up the mountain

Branches falling
Raindrops flying
Treetops swaying
People running
Big wind blowing
Hurricane! on the mountain.

A 📖 📝 **AZ** Look at another poem, from a different place.

First find Trinidad on the map of the Caribbean on page 77.

1 Read *Hurricane*, a poem by Dionne Brand, who lived in Trinidad as a child.
2 In your notebook list three signs in the weather that tell people that the hurricane is coming.
3 List three things people do to make their houses ready for the hurricane.
4 Look at the last verse again. Why do you think the people are running? Write your answer in your notebook.

B 📖 ⭐ *Hurricane* is a good poem to perform. Practise reading the poem aloud, using the **Tip** box to help you. Use your voice to make the meaning come alive. Perform the poem in a group.

Tip

Preparing to perform

• Make sure you understand what the poem means.
• Check that you can read all the words.
• Decide what kind of voice you will read with: Happy? Sad? Urgent? Slow?
• Think about how fast or how slowly you will read.
• Look for punctuation marks – they can help you to understand which words go together.
• Decide which words are the important ones in each line and make sure you say them clearly.

The Thunder is a Great Dragon

The thunder is a great dragon that lives in the water
and flies in the air.
He carries two stones.
When he strikes them together,
the lightning flashes and the thunder roars.
The dragon pursues the spirits of evil,
and wherever he finds them,
he slays them.
The evil spirits hide in the trees,
and the dragon destroys them.

A **AZ** This session focuses on a traditional poem from Mongolia.
First look at Mongolia on the map.

1 Read *The Thunder is a Great Dragon* poem. Then read the poem aloud with expression.

2 What do you know about Mongolia? Discuss the poem and how it is linked to Mongolia, the country it comes from.

3 Talk about what happens in the poem. Which words make pictures in your head?

Did you know?

Mongolia is a country in central Asia, between Russia and China. In Mongolian myths, dragons are linked to water, thunder, lightning and the power of the earth.

B Work in groups. Plan a short drama about the poem
The Thunder is a Great Dragon. Perform your drama.

C Now write your own poem – a short poem explaining another way the dragon could make thunder. Think of some powerful words and noun phrases to use in your poem. Remember that your poem doesn't need to rhyme.

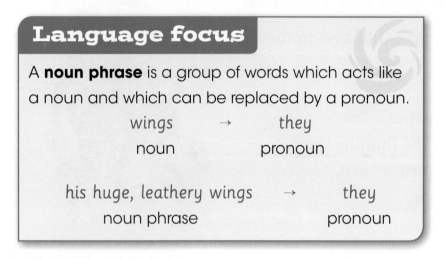

Language focus

A **noun phrase** is a group of words which acts like a noun and which can be replaced by a pronoun.

wings	→	they
noun		pronoun

his huge, leathery wings	→	they
noun phrase		pronoun

4 Animal songs

A This session is about a poem from Africa.

1 Look at the map, showing the Congo river and forests in central Africa.

2 Read the poem *Song of the Animal World* about the way animals move in the forest.

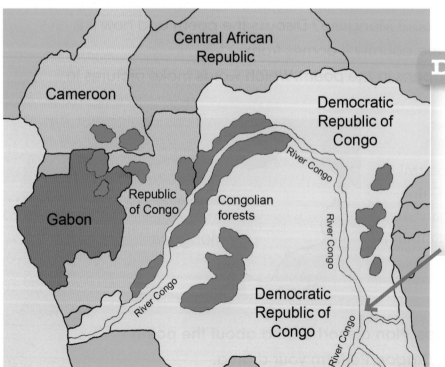

Did you know?

The Congo river is the deepest river in the world and the ninth longest river in the world. It wriggles through a huge rainforest with many colourful animals in it.

Song of the Animal World

Narrator: The fish goes
Chorus: Hip!
Narrator: The bird goes
Chorus: Viss!
Narrator: The monkey goes
Chorus: Gnan!

Fish: I start to the left,
I twist to the right.
I am the fish
That slips through the water,
That slides,
That twists,
That leaps!

Narrator: Everything lives,
Everything dances,
Everything sings.
Chorus: Hip! Viss! Gnan!

Bird: The bird flies away,
Flies, flies, flies,
Goes, returns, passes,
Climbs, floats, swoops.
I am the bird!

Narrator: Everything lives,
Everything dances,
Everything sings.
Chorus: Hip! Viss! Gnan!

Monkey: The monkey!
From branch to branch
Runs, hops, jumps,
With his wife and baby,
Mouth stuffed full, tail in air,
Here's the monkey!
Here's the monkey!

Narrator: Everything lives,
Everything dances,
Everything sings.
Chorus: Hip! Viss! Gnan!

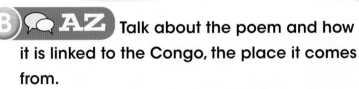

B 💬 **AZ** Talk about the poem and how it is linked to the Congo, the place it comes from.

1 Discuss the sounds in the poem. How has the poet created the animal sounds?

2 Talk about movement in the poem. What movement words are there? Do you think the poem is a happy poem or a sad one?

Notice how the verb endings change depending on the noun or pronoun the verb goes with:
I **twist** to the right.
The fish **twists** to the right.
I **sing**.
Everything **sings**.

You are going to make up another verse for the poem.

1 Copy the table below into your notebook. Fill it in with information from the poem about the bird and the monkey.

2 Think of another animal from Africa and write its name in the last row of the table. You could choose a frog, a giraffe, a crocodile or a leopard – or a different animal.

3 Make notes in the table about the sound it makes, where it lives and how it moves.

4 Write a new verse about your chosen animal.

Animal	How it sounds	Where it lives	How it moves	Other information
fish	Hip!	the water	twists, slips, slides, leaps	swims through the water
bird				
monkey				

5 Moving like a cat

Did you know?

Japan is made up of a string of more than six thousand islands in East Asia. It is sometimes called the Land of the Rising Sun because its name in Japanese means 'sun-origin'. Many Japanese people are very fond of cats – there is even a national cat day.

A 📖 ★ **AZ** Haikus are Japanese poems with 17 syllables and three lines. There are five syllables in the first and last lines, and seven syllables in the middle line. Haikus are very short but they try to paint a very clear picture of something.

1 Read the haiku about a cat. Count the syllables in each line.
2 Talk about how the haiku is linked to the country it is from.
  What can you say about the sounds in the poem?
3 Read the poem aloud with expression.

Suddenly awake.
Stretching, yawning, arching back,
stalking, pouncing: cat.

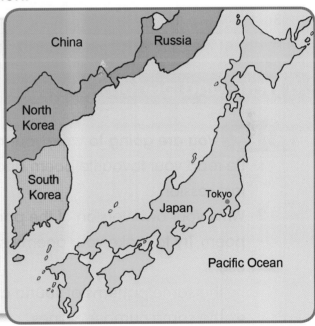

Language focus

The number of **syllables** in a word helps give it rhythm.
- The word *cat* has one syllable.
- *Awake* (a-wake) has two syllables and so does *stretching* (stret-ching).
- *Suddenly* (sud-den-ly) has three syllables – and so does *syllables* (syl-lab-les)!

B **Look back at the poems in this unit and choose three of them to compare.**

1 Copy the table into your notebook and fill it in with notes about each of your chosen poems.

2 Are there any links between the poems?

3 Which poem did you like best? Why?

4 Write a review of your favourite poem.

- Say what you liked about the poem.
- Explain how the poem is linked to the country it is from.
- Comment on the pictures the poem paints.
- Write about the powerful or unusual words the poet has chosen and the sounds they make.

	Title	Country	Topic	Language	Interesting things
1					
2					
3					

6 Write and perform a poem

A **You are going to write your own poem.**

1 Re-read your favourite poem and the review you wrote about it in the last session.

2 Write your own version of the poem, or add a new verse to the original poem. Try to make your poem as much like the original as you can. Use:

- the same patterns of sound and language
- the same number of lines
- the same kind of words.

B **★ AZ** **Now get ready to perform your poem.**

1 Read your poem aloud. Are there ways you can improve it?
Ask a talk partner to listen to you reading your poem and to suggest improvements you could make.

2 Practise reading your improved poem again and again.
  - Read with expression.
  - Use movement.
  - Use your voice and your body to support the poem's meaning.
3 Perform your poem.

How did I do?

In this unit you have read poems from around the world and explored how poets use words to make pictures and create sounds.

1 Read the start of a poem, *Coral Reef* by Clare Bevan.
2 Discuss these questions about the poem.
  - How is the poem linked to a place?
  - Is it linked to a country?
  - Which words in the poem help to make a picture in your head?

Coral Reef

I am a teeming city;

An underwater garden

Where fishes fly;

A lost forest

of skeleton trees;

A home for starry anemones;

A hiding places for frightened fishes;

A skulking place for prowling predators;

An alien world

Whose unseen monsters

Watch with luminous eyes.

D  ★ **Look again at** *Coral Reef.*

1 In your notebook write:
- three nouns that helped you to know about the place
- three adjectives that helped build up a picture of the place
- three different noun phrases from the poem.

2 Think how you would perform the poem.
- Do you know what all the words mean? How could you find the meanings of any words you don't know?
- Find the important words that you will say most clearly.
- Think about how the punctuation helps you.
- How fast or how slowly will you read the poem? What kind of voice will you read with?

3 Perform the poem in groups.

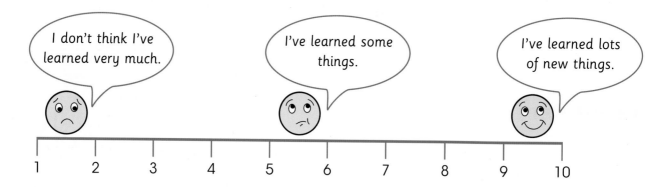

7 Dragons and pirates

In this unit you will look at different types of stories, especially adventure stories. You will learn more about characters, setting and plot. You will have a chance to act out an adventure story and write your own.

You will also learn about:
interesting words, pronouns, complex sentences, paragraphs and chapters, adverbs and adverbial phrases.

1 Adventures

A

B

C

D

A 💬 What are adventures? What are the children in the photos doing?

B 📖 ⭐ Listen as your teacher reads the play script. Then read the story yourself. Read it in a dull boring voice, then use a more interesting voice.

Lucas, Fernando and Ana are on a day out with their parents in the rainforest. They are at the pool they normally swim in. Their parents are chatting to some friends they have met.

Fernando: This is no good. There are too many people here.

Lucas: I expect they're from the coach we saw in the car park.

Ana: Let's go up the river and see if there's another pool for us.

Lucas: Wander off? Mum and Dad won't like that.

Fernando: No, they wouldn't! There are snakes and spiders! We might fall into the river, or trip over a branch, or get stung, or bitten. Anyway, we might get lost.

Ana: OK. You stay here with all these people. I'm going by myself!

(Ana starts to walk off. Lucas and Fernando look at each other.)

Lucas: Ana, come back! What shall we do, Fernando? We can't let her go by herself. We'd better go after her. Come on!

Fernando: I don't like this! What will happen to us?

Language focus

Look for the **punctuation marks** – they will help you understand the text and read with expression.

- Full stops show you where the end of the sentence is. You usually pause slightly between sentences.
- Question marks show you the end of the questions. What does your voice do when you ask a question?
- Exclamation marks show a sentence that must be read with expression. Match the expression to the meaning of the words. Is the character surprised? Excited? Bored? Worried? Determined? Angry?
- Commas are used to separate things in lists and to show which words go together in different sections of the sentence.

C **AZ** Answer these questions in your notebook.

1 What are the names of the characters in the play script?
2 Why are the children cross?
3 Why doesn't Lucas want to go further up the river?
4 What is Fernando worried about?
5 Write a sentence to describe the kind of person Ana is.

D ★ Act out the play script in groups. Then write some more of the play script to show what happens next.

2 Story beginnings

Did you know?

There are stories about dragons from all around the world. In stories from China and India, the dragons are usually long, like snakes, and have four feet. But in stories from Europe and America, the dragons are shorter and have legs and wings.

A 📖 💬 **AZ** Listen to and read these story beginnings. Which one makes you want to read more of the story? Which story do you think will be a good adventure story? How do you know these are all fiction texts?

1 My name is Alfie Small, and I'm a famous explorer. I have lots of dangerous adventures and always take my rucksack with me, just in case!

At the bottom of my garden, behind the rickety shed, is the special place I go exploring.

The grass grows long and the weeds are tall and I never know what I might find.

Today, I pushed through the weeds … and found a small boat floating on a small stream.

So I climbed aboard and paddled away.

Alfie Small

2 If you think this is the kind of story where five children, armed only with a bucket and spade, catch a dangerous band of smugglers, you'd be wrong. And if you think this is the kind of story where a poor helpless little girl is captured by a terrible gang of cut-throat pirates … you'd still be wrong, but a lot closer. Now, those are all the hints I'm going to give you. To find out what happens, you'd better read on …

Rose Impey

3 Lily licked the mixing spoon like a large lollipop. She asked, "Gran, why do they laugh at Granda sometimes?"

"Who laughs at your granda, my lovely?"

"People. They say he's strange."

"Well, he is different from the rest, Lily," said Gran. "That's why I married him."

Lily went out into the garden, through the gate and up the path to the hills. She found Granda sitting on a hump, whistling to himself.

"Granda, why do you like the hills so much?" asked Lily.

He smiled. "Because these are Dragon Hills."

"Real dragons?" asked Lily.

"Real sleeping dragons," said Granda. 'Would you like to hear how I came to know all about them?"

Pippa Goodhart

 **B** Copy these noun phrases into your notebook.

| a famous explorer | real sleeping dragons | a poor helpless little girl |

1 Using a coloured pencil, underline the adjective in each of the phrases.
2 Then, using a different coloured pencil, underline the nouns.
3 Are the adjectives before or after the nouns? Why do you think the writers used noun phrases instead of simple nouns?

Language focus

A **noun** is a word that names something. Words like *dragon*, *pirate* and *explorer* are all nouns.

A **noun phrase** is a group of words that act like a noun. In a noun phrase you always have a noun and you often have an adjective which describes the noun.

Now copy these sentences into your notebook.

- The grass is long and the weeds are tall.
- Dragons are long and scaly.
- Pirates are scary and brave.

1 Using a coloured pencil, underline all the adjectives.
2 Then, using a different coloured pencil, underline all the nouns. What do you notice about the position of the adjectives compared to the last activity?

3 What happens next?

Look at the exclamation marks! How will you read the sentences which finish with exclamation marks?

So I climbed aboard and paddled away. The stream got bigger and the water flowed faster, and soon I was racing along as fast as a speedboat.

I saw a huge boulder blocking the river. It was shaped like a dragon's head and my boat raced straight towards it. Help! I thought I was going to crash.

Then, with an awful grinding noise, the rock began to move. A dark cave opened up like a yawning mouth, and I was swept inside.

Whoosh! I whizzed along a gloomy tunnel, holding on tight as my boat zigzagged between rocks as sharp as dragon fangs.

The water roared and my boat spun round and round. Soon I couldn't tell which way was home.

Suddenly, I shot out of the tunnel and found myself floating on a choppy sea. In the distance was a small island, with a plume of smoke billowing up from behind some trees. I steered my boat towards it.

A 📖 📝 **AZ** Read the next part of Alfie's adventure on page 91.
Answer the questions in your notebook.

1 Did Alfie see a dragon in the water? Explain your answer.
2 Write the words Alfie uses to describe how the cave opened up.
3 What were the rocks inside the tunnel like?
4 Write five powerful words or phrases from the passage that tell you most about **where** Alfie was.
5 Write five powerful words or phrases from the passage that tell you most about **what** Alfie did.

B 💬 📝 What will happen next? Are there any clues in the text that help you guess what happens next? In your notebook, draw what you think will happen to Alfie. Label your drawing with:

• three words that tell you where Alfie was
• three words that tell you what Alfie saw
• three words that tell you what Alfie did.

C 📖 📝 Look at the **Language focus** box and then re-read the passage. Make a list in your notebook of the different pronouns you find.

Language focus

Pronouns can take the place of a noun or noun phrase in a sentence.
For example:
The famous explorer climbed into the famous explorer's boat.
→ **He** climbed into **his** boat or **I** climbed into **my** boat.
The angry pirates ran to the angry pirates' boat. →
They ran to **their** boat or **We** ran to **our** boat.

D 📖 Find the adjectives in the text on page 91. Are they used before or after the noun they describe?

4 Character portraits

Language focus

Simple sentences have one main verb – *Alfie Small* **was** *an explorer.*

Compound sentences are two simple sentences joined together with *and, but, so* or *or* – *Alfie Small* **got** *into his boat* **and** *he* **paddled** *away.*

Complex sentences have a main sentence joined to another part of a sentence by a range of words such as *because, if, that, although, when* and *until.* The part of the complex sentence after this word wouldn't be a sentence on its own. These are complex sentences:

Alfie **was** *worried* **because** *he* **was going** *to crash.*

(*Because he was going to crash* isn't a proper sentence.)

When *he* **saw** *the dragon, he* **was** *frightened.*

(*When he saw the dragon* isn't a proper sentence.)

(A) 💬 📝 **Would you like to be friends with Alfie Small? Talk with a talk partner about the sort of person he is. Then write a character portrait of Alfie Small.**

Tip

In your character portrait, use:

- interesting noun phrases to describe what Alfie looks like

- interesting verbs to describe what he thinks, does, says and writes

- different types of sentences in your writing.

Session 4 Character portraits   93

5 Chapter headings

A 📖💬 **AZ** Longer books are split into sections called **chapters**.

1 Why do you think writers use chapters?

2 Read these chapter headings from the book *Pirates and Dragons* by Alfie Small. Work with a talk partner, using the chapter headings to tell each other a story.

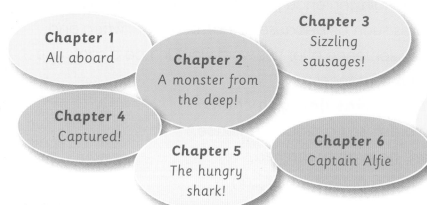

Chapter 1
All aboard

Chapter 2
A monster from the deep!

Chapter 3
Sizzling sausages!

Chapter 4
Captured!

Chapter 5
The hungry shark!

Chapter 6
Captain Alfie

Reading the chapter headings is a good way of seeing whether you will like a book. You can often guess the kind of book it is from the chapter headings.

B 📝 Copy these sentences into your notebook. Choose an adverb or adverbial phrase from the box to begin each new sentence.

> At the end   All at once   Behind his shed   Carefully   Early one morning
> Joyfully   To his surprise   When he was ready

1 … Alfie left his house and walked down his garden path.
2 … he found a stream.
3 … there was a boat.
4 … he climbed into the boat.
5 … he started to paddle.

When an adverb comes at the beginning of a sentence, some people like to separate it from the rest of the sentence with a comma.

Language focus

A phrase is a group of words.

A phrase which tells you more about a verb is called an **adverbial phrase**.

For example, *as quickly as possible, later that evening, outside the house* are all adverbial phrases.

6 A story about Alfie

Today, I pushed through the weeds … and found a big, stripy balloon with a wicker basket hanging underneath.

"Come on, Jed!" I cried, jumping into the basket. I untied a rope, and the balloon rose high into the sky.

Thick, shifting clouds loomed before us. They formed into the shape of a monstrous ogre's face. Its grinning mouth opened wide and we were swept inside. Jed began to whine.

"Oh, help! Watch out, boy," I cried, as our balloon was buffeted about, and we were thrown around the basket like clothes in a washing machine. Soon I couldn't tell which way was home.

Suddenly, we went spinning out of the cloud. Below us, everything had changed and now we were floating above a strange, rocky landscape.

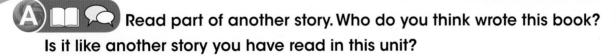

A 📖💬 Read part of another story. Who do you think wrote this book? Is it like another story you have read in this unit?

B 📝 Answer these questions in your notebook.
1 What was behind the weeds?
2 Who do you think Jed is?
3 What did the cloud look like?
4 What did Jed do when the balloon went into the ogre's mouth?
5 Did you guess that the story is another story about Alfie Small?
6 Which creatures do you think Alfie will meet in this adventure?

 **Plan your own Alfie Small adventure.**
- Start by writing the chapter headings.
- Tell a talk partner the story you plan to write.
- Start to write your story.

7 Dragon Boy

Here, Granda is telling Lily about his father's experience in the Dragon Hills.

"You see, Lily, the villagers needed fire to warm their homes, and cook their food, and make life good. So they chose the biggest, bravest man in the village. They gave him a fine spear and they called him Fire Snatcher.
My da, your great-granda, Lily, was Fire Snatcher and hero of the village."

"But how did he snatch the fire?" asked Lily.

"Well, Lily, dragons are strange creatures," said Granda. "They lay their eggs, then sleep for a full ninety years until the eggs are ready to hatch. When that happens, the dragon mothers wake up to care for their babies. The dragons were in their sleep-years when my da was Fire Snatcher. All he had to do was creep, tiptoe-quiet into the hills, then jump, suddenly, on a sleeping dragon and poke it with his spear.

"The poor beast would start from its sleep and blaze with fright, just as you or I would if anybody jabbed at us with a needle while we were sleeping. But it worked. It made the dragon roar fire. As it roared, the Fire Snatcher thrust his torch of dry wood into the flare of the dragon's fiery breath to light it."

A 📖 📝 **AZ** Read another passage from *Dragon Boy.* (You read the start of the story on page 90.) Then answer these questions in your notebook.

1 List two things the villagers needed fire for.
2 How did the villagers choose the Fire Snatcher?
3 Why did the Fire Snatcher need a spear?
4 What did the Fire Snatcher do when the dragon roared?
5 Why do you think the Fire Snatcher needed to be brave?

B 💬 How is this adventure story the same as the ones about Alfie Small? How is it different?

C ⭐ Do a role play. Be a Fire Snatcher! Imagine you have to go out at night to get fire from sleeping dragons.

● What do you see, hear, smell, feel?
● What do you do? How do you move?

D 💬 With a partner, discuss these questions and decide on your answers.

1 Do you think this text is from a chapter near the beginning or near the end of the story?
2 Do you think the end of this text would be a good place to start a new chapter?

8 Setting and dialogue

A 📖 📝 **AZ** Re-read the passage from *Dragon Boy.* What did the Fire Snatcher see, hear and feel when he was in the Dragon Hills? Write a paragraph describing the setting for a story about dragons.

Language focus

Punctuate speech correctly.
● Use a new line for each speaker.
● Put " at the beginning of the words that were said.
● Put " at the end of them.
● Put question marks and exclamation marks before the closing speech marks.
● Don't forget capital letters and full stops.

B 💬 📝 Look again at the passage from *Dragon Boy*. Look at the **Language focus** box on page 97.

1 Discuss these questions.
- How many people speak?
- How do you know when they start to speak? And when they finish?
- How many times can you see the word *said*?
- Which other word is used instead of *said*?
- Suggest a different word that could have been used instead.

2 Copy this passage into your notebook with the correct punctuation. Some punctuation marks are missing, others are wrong. Write a word you could use instead of *said* in each of the gaps.

"Who was Dragon Boy? ___ Lily

Well, Lily," ___ Granda, there was a big fire and the villagers ran away

A mother dragon went to see if her eggs had hatched. what do you think she saw

I don't know, said Lily

she found one ordinary baby dragon and another baby he was pink and soft instead of green and scaly

I bet he was Dragon Boy, ___ Lily

9 More about paragraphs

A 📖 📝 **AZ** Read more of the story of Dragon Boy.
Then answer these questions in your notebook.

1 Why did Dragon Boy go off by himself?
2 How did he first make fire?
3 As he made the fire, what did he see?
4 What did he smell?
5 What did he hear?
6 What did he feel?
7 Dragon Boy could do something unusual to make the fire grow. What was it?
8 Which paragraph do you think is the most exciting? Why?

Here, Dragon Boy is growing up as a dragon, but he can't make fire. He just whistles.

1 One day, when Dragon Boy had been huffing and puffing nothing but whistles, some young dragons began laughing at him. Dragon Boy went off sadly on his own.

2 As the sun began to set, Dragon Boy turned for home. But he was still so cross that he kicked angrily at the flint stones under his feet. As one struck another, Dragon Boy saw a flash of yellow.

"Fire!" shouted Dragon Boy. "I've made fire without having to breathe it!"

3 Quickly he began collecting dry grass and sticks and bigger logs. Then, crouching down with his back to the wind, he struck two sharp flints, one against the other. CLACK! At first the stones just smelled a little smoky.

4 CLACK! CLACK! CLACK! He struck them again and again, until at last a spark flashed and took to the grass. As the grass smouldered and smoked, Dragon Boy blew on it gently. He sang a fiery dragon song, and suddenly the smouldering flowered into flames.

B Re-read the text and look at the **Language focus** box. Decide why the writer started new paragraphs when she did.

Language focus

Writers usually begin a new paragraph when they introduce a different action, a different time or a different place.
They often use an **adverb** or **adverbial phrase** at the beginning of a paragraph to tell the reader when, where or how the events take place.

A **AZ** Would you like to read an Alfie Small book or the *Dragon Boy* book? Explain why.

B Write a review of a non-fiction book you have enjoyed reading.

In your review, say:

- what you thought about the book when you read it
- what information was given in the book
- why the reader might want to read the book.

> A storyboard is a plan. Cartoons and other films are always planned as a series of pictures on a storyboard.

One day

In bed

The next day

After a week

Sadly

Tip

You could use a different chapter to write about each event in your story.

C Make your own dragon adventure storyboard like the one above. Use six boxes and draw your main characters in the top box. In boxes 1–5, draw pictures to show the main events.

Write an adverb or adverbial phrase for each picture.

11 Write a story

A 💬AZ Look at the storyboard you used to plan your adventure story in the previous session. Tell your story to a talk partner. How could you improve your story?

B 📝 When you are sure of your story, write it. Remember to:
- follow your storyboard, making sure you link the events
- start a new chapter at the beginning of a new event
- use paragraphs
- use different kinds of sentences and connectives
- use adverbs and adverbial phrases to show the order of the events and how they are linked
- say what your character sees, hears and does
- include some dialogue and powerful words.

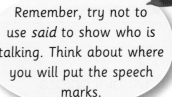

Remember, try not to use said to show who is talking. Think about where you will put the speech marks.

12 Improve your story

A 📖📝 Re-read the story you wrote in the previous session.
Are you pleased with it? Read it aloud to yourself or with a talk partner. As you read, check your spelling and punctuation and make sure you haven't missed any little words.
- Find three nouns that you could improve by choosing a better word or by adding an adjective to make a noun phrase.
- Look just at the verbs and think about the tense you used. Have you used the past tense to talk about events in the past?
- Do the verbs match the nouns or pronouns?

B 📝AZ Look at the list in Activity B in the last session. Change at least three more things in your writing to make sure you have done everything as well as you could.

How did I do?

C 💬 In this unit you have looked at adventure stories. What makes a good adventure story? What kind of setting do you need? What kind of characters do you need?

D 📝 Copy the table into your notebook and fill it in with the missing types of word and more examples.

Type of word	Examples
	dragon, pirate, boat, …
noun phrase	a fiery dragon, …
	I, he, she, it, us, …
	quickly, suddenly, later, …
adverbial phrase	all at once, …

E 📝 Join these pairs of sentences to make compound or complex sentences. Write your sentences in your notebook. Use different ways of joining the sentences each time.

1 The dragon had scales. It had wings.
2 The dragon was green. The boy was not.
3 The boy was sad. He wasn't like the dragons.
4 The boy was happy. He made fire.

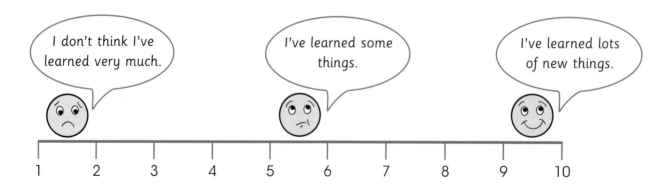

I don't think I've learned very much.

I've learned some things.

I've learned lots of new things.

1 2 3 4 5 6 7 8 9 10

8 Wonderful world

In this unit you will look at different types of non-fiction texts to find out about places. You will explore the language and features of information texts and work in a group to plan and give your own talk. At the end of the unit you will write an information text.

You will also learn about:

finding books in libraries, browsing, skimming and scanning, compound and complex sentences and connectives, matching verbs with nouns or pronouns, paragraphs in non-fiction texts.

1 Holidays

A 💬 📝 **Where do you go on holiday? What do you like doing on holiday? Write a short text about something that happened when you were on holiday. Describe the place as well as the event.**

Holiday fact file

Canada is a great place for winter sports, but people also come here for the clean air and awesome scenery.

The city of Vancouver is surrounded on three sides by water and on the fourth by mountains. It also has beautiful buildings.

South Africa attracts many holidaymakers, who come for its beaches and countryside, and for the safaris that allow visitors to see African animals in the wild.

With the flat-topped Table Mountain in the background, the city of Cape Town is famous for its harbour.

The Caribbean is a line of tiny countries with some of the best weather and the best beaches in the world.

Many cruise ships bring thousands of people to visit the islands.

Brazil has some great beaches and the city of Rio de Janeiro is famous for its carnival in the spring, when everyone dresses up and dances through the streets.

Brazil is perhaps most famous for the Amazon rainforest where visitors can see enormous trees, the river Amazon and some of the rarest and most beautiful creatures on the planet.

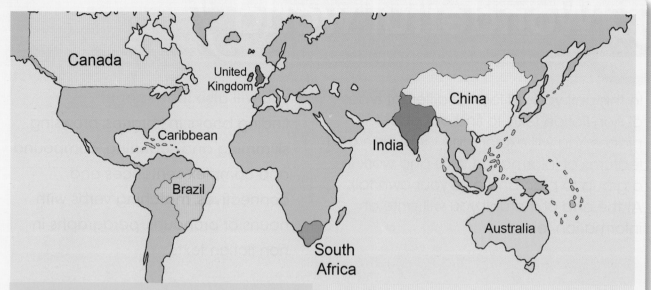

Australia is famous for its beaches. Many people in Australia enjoy surfing.

Australia also has the Great Barrier Reef, the world's largest coral reef system. People come from all over the world to scuba dive or snorkel and to admire the fish.

India is a land of contrasts with plenty to see. In the north are the mountains of the Himalayas and in the south are beautiful beaches. In between, people can visit modern cities and ancient temples, and see farmers farming the land as they have done for centuries.

China is an exciting place to visit. People come for its culture and history as well as its huge, modern cities.

The Great Wall of China is over 2000 years old and stretches over 8850 km (5500 miles). Many visitors come to walk on the wall and admire the views from it.

The United Kingdom is a little country with a lot of history. People come here to see the beautiful scenery in Scotland and Northern Ireland, ancient castles in Wales, and cities and many historical monuments in England.

B 📖 📝 **AZ** Read about the countries on this page and on page 103 and answer these questions in your notebook.

1 Which place is a line of small countries?
2 Which countries do people visit for the beaches?
3 What is Brazil most famous for?
4 Which countries would you visit to admire the scenery?
5 Which countries would you visit to see interesting creatures?
6 Which of the places would you like to go to on holiday?
   Explain why, using information from the book.

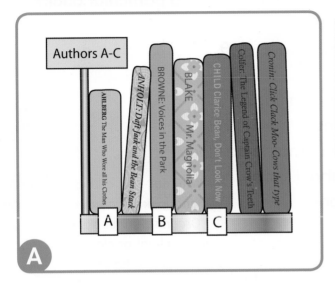

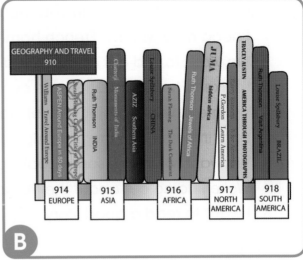

A 💬 **AZ** **Look at these shelves of books in a library.**

a Which books are fiction and which are non-fiction?

b How do you know?

c How are the books organised?

d Where would you look to find a book about where you live?

The Dewey Decimal system

This is how we organise the non-fiction books in our library. Look for the numbers on the spine of the books.

000–099	for general subjects
100–199	for philosophy
200–299	for religion
300–399	for social sciences
400–499	for language
500–599	for science
600–699	for technology
700–799	for arts and leisure
800–899	for literature
900–999	for history and geography

Did you know?

The Dewey Decimal system is a way of classifying or organising books using numbers. It lets you find a book more easily. For example, you will find science books in the 500s section. The science section is divided again, using numbers, into various subjects – books on plants (580–589) or animals (590–599), for example. Then these are subdivided into topics – such as fish (597) or birds (598).

B 📖 📝 Read the poster on page 105 about books in a school library.
What are the numbers you need to look for if you want a particular book?
Answer these questions in your notebook.

1 I need help with my French homework. 400–499
2 We want to find out about Africa.
3 I'd like to know about the life cycle of a frog.
4 We are doing a project on religions.
5 I am interested in the paintings of Leonardo da Vinci.
6 We want to borrow some books about space.
7 We're finding out about the Romans.
8 I want to read a good story.

> Why not visit a library
> and look for a book?
> Organise the books in
> your school or class and
> make a library.

C 📝 Write these authors in alphabetical order in
your notebook. Organise them using their family name.

Jon Scieszka · Rose Impey · Jacqueline Wilson · Alfie Smith · Martin Waddell · Michael Morpurgo · Ann Fine · Tony Ross · Jill Murphy · Laurence Anholt · Eoin Colfer · A.A. Milne · Colin McNaughton · Pippa Goodhart

Tip

If two people's names begin with the same letter, look at the second letters and put them in alphabetical order too.
For example, Elizabeth KAy comes before Rosalind KErven.

3 Inside a non-fiction book

1 Contents

2 Index

A 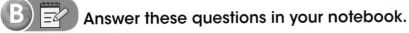 **Look at the texts. They are from a book about Caribbean islands. Where in the book would you find these pages? How are they organised?**

> The **contents** page tells you the main headings and topics in the book.
> The **index** tells you where to find out about particular subjects, names or ideas.

B **Answer these questions in your notebook.**

1 Which page would you look at to find information about volcanoes?

2 Which topic is on pages 10–11?

3 Which subjects, names or ideas can you find out more about on those pages?

4 Which sports do they play in the Caribbean?

5 What do you think page 17 is about?

6 Puerto Rico is discussed under two topics. What are they?

C **AZ** Non-fiction books give information in lots of different ways. Look at the fact file. Browse some non-fiction books and find the different features. Talk about what you find with a talk partner.

Fact file

Non-fiction texts

- The **heading** tells you what the topic is.

- The **text** gives information about the topic.

- If the text is quite long, **subheadings** tell you where the different bits of the topic are talked about.

- The **photographs**, **illustrations** and **diagrams** give you information using pictures not words.

- A **caption** is a short explanation of what is in a picture.

- A **label** names part of a diagram.

- Some of the information might be given in a **list**, with or without **bullet points**.

- There might be a **glossary** to tell you what some of the difficult words mean.

Language focus

Browsing means having a quick look through something, without spending time reading all of the words carefully. Here are some ways to browse a book.

- Look at the covers. What can you learn from the title? The pictures? The blurb?
- Open the book and quickly read the contents page.
- Flick through the book, looking at the pictures.

Browsing lets you get an idea of what the book is about so that you can decide whether you want to read it.

4 Skimming and scanning

 AZ Read this text aloud.
How do you read it?
Did you skim, scan or read
slowly and carefully?

There are two seasons in the Caribbean: a wet season and a dry season. Each season lasts for about six months.

The wet season is the season of rain. The wet season starts in about June and goes on until November. The rain is usually heavier inland, nearer the mountains.

During the wet season there are more tropical storms and hurricanes. Hurricanes are very, very strong winds, with heavy rain. There are usually about eight hurricanes each year.

There is less rain during the dry season which lasts from December to May. Tourists come to the islands then to enjoy the beautiful Caribbean beaches in the hot sun.

> There are different ways of reading.
> • **Skim** a text to get the main idea.
> • **Scan** to find a particular word or piece of information.
> • **Read slowly and carefully** to understand the text fully.

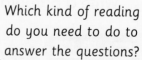 **B** Answer these questions in your notebook.

1 How many times can you find the words
   a *season* (or *seasons*),
   b *hurricane* (or *hurricanes*),
   c *Caribbean*?

2 When is the dry season?

3 Where is rain heaviest on the islands?

4 When do hurricanes occur? How many of them are there each year?

5 If you were going to the Caribbean, which month of the year would you like to go in? Why?

> Which kind of reading do you need to do to answer the questions?

C 💬 📝 Look at a non-fiction book with a talk partner. Write questions for each other about the information in the book. Do you have to use different kinds of reading to find the answers?

D 📝 Choose the correct verb and write the complete sentences in your notebook.

1 Whales (*swim/swims*) in the waters of the South Pacific Ocean near Chile.

2 They (*pass/passes*) Chile as they (*look/looks*) for food.

3 A boat (*take/takes*) people out to sea. They (*want/wants*) to see the whales.

4 Other animals (*live/lives*) in Chile too.

5 The Atacama desert (*is/are*) in Chile. It (*is/are*) the driest place on Earth.

6 At night, reptiles (*burrow/burrows*) underground in the desert. In the day, they (*lie/lies*) on rocks and (*get/gets*) warm.

5 Using paragraphs

A 📖 💬 Re-read the text about weather in the last session. Why is it divided into paragraphs? What is the main idea in each paragraph? Look at some more non-fiction books. Find the main idea in some of the paragraphs.

B 📝 Choose a topic you know about.

1 Think of **two** different ideas you would like to write about that topic.

2 Write a paragraph about each of the ideas.

> A new paragraph usually means there is a new subject or idea.

C 📝 **AZ** Copy these sentence beginnings into your notebook. Write the end of the sentences.

1 I would like to visit the Caribbean because

2 There are lovely white beaches and

3 It is beautiful in the dry season so

4 It rains hard in the mountains but

Language focus

A **simple sentence** has only one verb. For example, *Many tourists visit the Caribbean in the dry season.*

You know that sentences can be joined by little words such as *and, but, so, because* and *when.* These joining words are called **connectives**.

Compound sentences are two simple sentences joined together with the connectives *and, so, but* or *or.*

Complex sentences have a main sentence joined to another part of a sentence by connectives such as *because, although, until* or *when.*

6 Language features of information texts

The centre of Australia is a huge desert called the Outback. It is very dry and flat with red earth. In the middle of the outback there is a town called Alice Springs. Many tourists visit Alice Springs because they want to see the mountain-sized rock nearby.

It has two official names: Uluru and Ayers Rock. Uluru is the traditional Aboriginal name for it. Ayers Rock is the English name given to it in the 19th century.

A 📖 📝 **AZ** **Read the paragraph about Australia. Then answer these questions in your notebook.**

1 What is the main idea in this paragraph?
2 What heading would you give it?
3 Which tense is the writing in?
4 Write one fact from the text.

Did you know?

People have lived near Uluru for over ten thousand years.

It is one piece of sandstone rock.

It is about 3.6 km long and 1.9 km wide.

The climb to the top is over 1.6 km, up a steep slope. The top of the rock is quite flat.

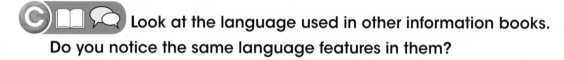 **B** Talk about the language used in the text. What tense is it written in? Are there any powerful verbs? What about interesting adjectives – are there any? Answer these questions in your notebook.

1 Find the verbs in the text. Which verb is used most?

2 Find the adjectives in the text. Write them in your notebook. Do they help give more facts?

3 Now look for the pronouns in the text. Can you find the pronouns *I, you* or *we*? Which pronouns can you find?

4 What punctuation can you find in the text? Are there any question marks or exclamation marks? Why do you think this is?

C Look at the language used in other information books. Do you notice the same language features in them?

7 Non-fiction e-texts

Fact file

An e-text is an electronic text – that just means it's a text on a screen, not in a book. You will find most of the same text features in non-fiction e-texts as you do in non-fiction books. Here are some features you only find in e-texts:

- You may be able to hear the text read aloud.
- You may be able to look at videos as well as photographs.
- If you click on a highlighted word or image, you may be shown more information about it.
- You can print the screen – and you may be able to add your own notes to the text first.
- You may be able to email the text to your friends.

A When have you used an e-text to find information? Look at the fact file. Talk about the features of e-texts with a talk partner as you look at information on web pages together.

> You find e-texts on the internet, or on CD-ROMs or DVDs, and you read them on computers, tablets, e-book readers or mobile phones.

B Look at a non-fiction e-text and a non-fiction book. Then talk about these questions.

- Are the paragraphs used in the same way?
- Can you skim and scan the e-text to find information quickly? What about with the book?
- Is the way that you find the information the same in both texts?

Did you know?

Use the internet safely.

- Make sure an adult can see what you are doing.
- Ask an adult before you visit any new websites.
- Ask for help if you're not sure what to do.
- Never give your full name, your school or your address on the internet.
- Tell an adult if you see or read anything that makes you feel uncomfortable.

The internet is useful and fun if you use it safely.

8 Plan a talk

A You are going to find out about a subject and give a talk about it.

1 Work in a group and choose a subject for your talk.
2 Split the subject into topics and decide who will research which topic.
3 Look at the table on page 114. Can you see how the subject has been split into topics? Copy a blank version of the table into your notebook and write in the subject your group has chosen and the topic you are going to research.
4 Then write some questions to find out about.

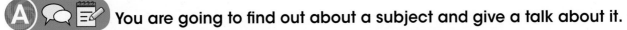

Subject: NORWAY	
Topics and questions	**Answers**
1 Geography Where is it? Which other countries are nearby?	In northern Europe – Scandinavia Sweden, Denmark, Finland, Poland, Germany, UK
2 Cities What is the capital city? What do people go and see in the cities?	Oslo. Nearly 800,000 people live there Viking ship museum – Vikings came from Norway Sculpture park People don't usually go there for the cities
3 Countryside What does it look like? What do people do in the countryside?	Lots of fjords (say fee-ords) where the sea goes far inland The north is in the Arctic Circle with reindeer (called caribou); it's the land of the midnight sun because the sun doesn't set in summer Skiing in winter Whale watching in the Atlantic Climb glaciers (frozen rivers or masses of ice)

B 📖 📝 **Do your research.**

Use books and e-texts to find the information you need.
Make notes of interesting information in the 'Answers'
column of your table.

When you look for information, decide if
you need to skim, scan or read carefully.

9 Give your talk

A 💬 Before you present your talk, practise giving it with your group. Work together to improve the talk. Give your talk to the class. Try to answer any questions your listeners ask at the end.

Tip

When you give a talk:

- begin with a clear statement about what the talk will be about
- introduce each part of the talk separately, with its own heading
- talk mostly in the present tense
- use the language of the texts you have met in this unit
- try to give information your listeners will be interested in and make your voice interesting too
- speak clearly and confidently, making eye contact with your listeners.

> Don't forget to say what the subject of your talk is first. Enjoy yourself when you give your talk!

B ⭐ Listen politely and with interest to the other talks. Sit still and quietly so you can listen carefully. Think of some questions you could ask at the end.

10 Plan an information text

A 📖 Look back at the texts in this unit. What is the same about them? What is different? Look at:

- the type of information they give
- the language
- how they are organised into paragraphs
- the headings, subheadings, pictures, captions and labels.

B 📝 Decide on a country to write an information text about. How will you record your research? You could use a mind map or a table like the one on page 114. Draw your plan.

 Research your subject using books and e-texts.

11 Write an information text

Remember how you researched
the talk you gave in the previous session.
Use the skills you learned from doing that.

A ★ 💬 Look at the planning sheet you
used in the previous session. Read your text aloud to a talk partner
and ask them to tell you how to improve it. Make sure you include
interesting things the readers will want to know about.

B 📝 **AZ** Write your information text. Use a computer if you can.
Remember to:
- follow your plan
- write in paragraphs, starting a new paragraph for each new topic or idea
- use headings for your paragraphs
- give interesting information
- use simple, compound and complex sentences with different connectives
- keep the tense the same and make sure the nouns and pronouns match
  the verbs.

C 💬 Which country did you write about? Can you find it on the map on
page 104?

12 Improve your text

A 📖 **AZ** Re-read your information text from the previous session. Are
you pleased with it? Why or why not? Read it aloud to yourself. As you read,
check the following and change your writing if you need to.
1 Check your spelling and punctuation and make sure you haven't missed
  out any little words.
2 Have you used good headings in the right places?
3 Do you need to add new information or move information to a
  different paragraph?
4 Look at the verbs. Have you used the present tense all the way through?
  Do the verbs match the nouns or pronouns?
5 Are there any sentences that you could join together?

B 📝 When you have checked everything, present your text attractively for display. Check it through again to make sure it is as good as possible.

How did I do?

C 💬 In this unit you have looked at non-fiction information texts.
1 What is the difference between paragraphs in stories and paragraphs in information texts?
2 What is the difference between the language in stories and the language in information texts?
3 What are the most important things to remember when writing information texts?

D 📝 Use connectives to join the pairs of sentences. Use a different connective each time. Write your sentences in your notebook.
1 In Australia the cities are near the coast. There are lots of beaches.
2 Alice Spring is near Uluru. People stay in hotels in Alice Springs.
3 Hurricanes happen in the Caribbean. People still go to the islands.
4 Chile sometimes has earthquakes. It sometimes has tsunamis too.
5 Penguins live on the coast of Chile. Not many people see them.

E 📝 Choose the correct verb to go with the nouns or pronouns. Then write the sentences in your notebook.
1 Whales (*swim*/*swims*) in the South Atlantic.
2 They (*are*/*is*) feeding.
3 People (*go*/*goes*) out in boats to watch them.
4 They sometimes (*have*/*has*) to travel a long way.
5 Whales (*travels*/*travel*) even further.

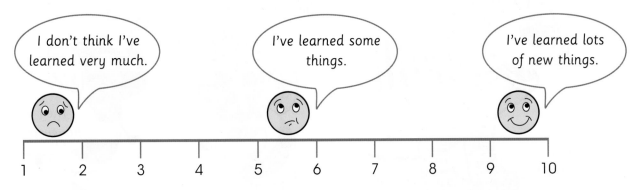

I don't think I've learned very much.

I've learned some things.

I've learned lots of new things.

1 2 3 4 5 6 7 8 9 10

9 Laughing allowed

In this unit you will think about different ways of playing with words. You will read jokes and different kinds of funny poems and think about what makes them funny. Then you will write your own funny poem.

You will also learn about:
puns, the past tense.

1 Jokes

A 💬 **What makes you laugh? Things you see? Things you hear? Talk about what makes something funny. Which of these jokes do you think is the funniest? Why?**

What do you call a dinosaur that's a noisy sleeper?

A bronto-snorus!

Baa.

Moo.

Yes, I'm learning a foreign language.

Did you say Baa?

Which side of a tiger has more stripes?

The outside!

Why do bees have sticky hair?

They use honeycombs.

B  **Read these jokes. Explain the puns in them.**

Do you know other jokes with puns?

Language focus

A **pun** is a play on words. Puns use a word that has several meanings or that sounds like another word. They work because you expect the word to mean one thing but then it turns out to mean something else. For example:

- a honeycomb is something you find in a beehive but a comb is also something you comb your hair with
- a side often means the left or the right but it is also part of *inside* or *outside*
- a bank can mean somewhere you keep your money but it can also be the side of a river.

Other puns work because you change a word or part of one to sound like another. So instead of *brontosaurus* you have the made-up word *bronto-snorous* – the *snore* bit makes you think of someone who snores.

Where do wise fish keep their money?

In a river bank.

What flies all day but never gets anywhere?

A flag.

What can you never make right, no matter how hard you try?

Your left foot.

Language focus

A **homonym** is a word that looks the same as another word but has a different meaning. Some puns work because of homonyms.

C ✎ **AZ** Read about homonyms in the **Language box** above.

1 Copy this list of homonyms into your notebook. Beside each word write two sentences that show two different meanings of the word.

> bark   bat   light   sink   watch

2 Find the homonyms in Activity B.

2 Wordplay

Wordspinning

Spin pins into nips.
Snap pans into naps.
Mix spit into tips.
Turn parts into traps.

Switch post into stop.
Whisk dear into dare.
Carve hops into shop.
Rip rate into tear.

Twist tame into mate.
Make mean into name.
Juggle taste into state
In the wordspinning game.

John Foster

Teeth

"Your teeth are like the stars," he said

And pressed her hand so white.

He spoke the truth for, like the stars,

Her teeth came out at night.

A 📖 ⭐ Read the poems on page 120 and think about the different ways they play with words. Choose the poem you like best. Practise reading it aloud until you can recite it without having to read it.

B 📝 Answer these questions in your notebook.

1 In *Wordspinning*, what is the same about the words *mean* and *name*?

2 Find two words the poet uses with the same letters as *spin*.

3 In *Teeth*, how were her teeth like the stars?

4 Was he trying to be kind or unkind when he said her teeth were like stars? How do you know?

Language focus

The **past tense** form of **regular verbs** ends in **ed** – for example *danc**ed**, ask**ed**, play**ed**, sort**ed** and tri**ed**.*

Other verbs, called **irregular verbs**, don't follow this rule and have different past tense forms.

C 📖 📝 **AZ** Scan the poem *Teeth* to find verbs in the past tense. Write down the verbs. One is a regular past tense verb (ending in **ed**) and three are irregular past tense verbs.

3 Funny poems and limericks

A 📖 💬 Read the poems. Talk about why they are funny.

I Built a Fabulous Machine

I built a fabulous machine
to keep my room completely clean.
It swept it up in nothing flat –
has anybody seen the cat?

Jack Prelutsky

Meow?

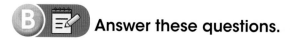 **B** **Answer these questions.**

1 Why was the machine *fabulous*?
2 What do you think *nothing flat* means in *I Built a Fabulous Machine*?
3 Why is the last line of *I Built a Fabulous Machine* funny?
4 Write three of the adjectives that describe monsters in *The Monster*.
5 Why is the last line of *The Monster* funny?

C **Read the limerick *There Was an Old Man with a Beard*. Then talk about what makes it a funny poem.**

The Monster

Some are ugly,
Some are tall,
Some are scary,
Some are small.
Some are difficult to see.
And some are in my family.

Emma Hjeltnes

Did you know?

Edward Lear wrote this poem. It is called a limerick. Edward Lear wrote his poems more than 150 years ago. He wrote lots of limericks and nonsense poems. He was also a good artist.

There Was an Old Man With a Beard

There was an old man with a beard
Who said, "It is just as I feared! –
Two owls and a hen,
Four larks and a wren,
Have all built their nests in my beard!"

D 💬 **AZ** Look at the limerick with gaps.

1 Decide with a talk partner what other words could complete the lines of the limerick.

2 Choose the three most important words from the poem. Explain why you chose them.

> There was _____ with a beard
> Who said, "_____ I feared!
> _____ and a hen,
> _____ and a wren,
> _____ in my beard!"

Language focus

A **limerick** is a funny poem of five lines. All limericks have the same rhythm and rhyme pattern: lines 1, 2 and 5 rhyme, and lines 3 and 4 rhyme.

Choosing words in poems is even more difficult than choosing words in stories. As well as making sense and telling the readers what you want them to know, words in poems also have to:

- fit the rhythm of the poem
- fit the rhyme of the poem (if there is one).

Any volunteers? Do you know any more limericks?

4 Calligrams and mnemonics

A 📖 📝 Read the poem. Why do you think the poet wrote her poem in this shape? Answer these questions in your notebook.

1 Why had someone made the kite?

2 What does *attain a great height* mean?

3 What happened to the kite?

4 What do you think will happen next?

Kite

> I'm
> part of a
> project on flight.
> I'm supposed to attain
> a great height. But
> unfortunately
> I got stuck
> in a tree
> so
> it
> looks
> like
> I'm
> here
> for
> the
> night!

Language focus

Kite is a **calligram**. A calligram is a poem or word arranged on the page to make a picture. The picture shows the theme of the poem or the meaning of the word.

B 💬 Talk about these calligram words. How could calligrams help you to remember spellings and meanings?

stretch

gleam drop

Language focus

A **mnemonic** is a saying which helps you to remember the spelling of a word or a fact.

C 📖💬 Read the mnemonics. Do you think they would be helpful?

because = **b**ig **e**lephants **c**an **a**lways **u**nderstand **s**maller **e**lephants.

points of the compass – North, East, South and West = **N**aughty **E**lephants **S**quirt **W**ater.

friend = A really good fri**end** stays right until the **end**.

said = **S**ally-**A**nne **is d**ancing.

D ✏️ **AZ** Write a mnemonic to help you to remember how to spell one of these words.

> want   eight   was   laugh

5 Write a poem

A 📖 ⭐ Read the tongue-twisters. Read each one three times, as fast as you can.

She sells seashells on the seashore.

Peter Piper picked a peck of pickled peppers.

Red lorry, yellow lorry. Red lolly, yellow lolly.

B 📝 💬 Why do you think they are called tongue-twisters? Write a definition of a tongue-twister in your notebook.

C 📖 📝 **AZ** Re-read the different poems and examples of wordplay in this unit. Plan and write your own poem based on one of the poems.

Alliteration is when you use the same sound at the beginning of several words that are close together. You all know that I am a delightfully daring, dazzling duck! What are you?

6 Perform your poem

A 📖 ⭐ Read your poem to a talk partner. Can they help you to improve it? Think about:

- the wordplay
- the sounds of the words
- the rhythm and rhyme
- your choice of words – could you choose better adjectives or stronger verbs?

Don't forget to check your spelling!

B ⭐ Practise performing your poem. Read it aloud several times, thinking about the sounds, rhythm, rhyme and meaning. When you are happy with it, perform your poem.

How did I do?

C 💬 In this unit you have read jokes, poems with puns and poems that played with the sounds in words. You have read funny poems, limericks, calligrams and mnemonics. You have even got your tongue round some tongue-twisters. Which type of poem used:

- rhythm?
- rhyme?
- puns?
- sounds?

What else was important in these poems and wordplays?

D 💬 Which type of poem did you find easiest to perform? Why?

- Did you enjoy the performance?
- What went well?
- What could have been even better?

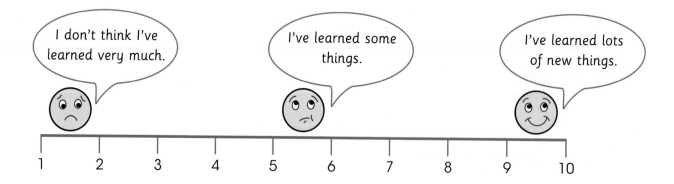

I don't think I've learned very much.

I've learned some things.

I've learned lots of new things.

1 2 3 4 5 6 7 8 9 10

Term 1 Spelling activities

(A) AZ Compound words

Compound words are words made up of two shorter words:

break + fast = breakfast   tooth + brush = toothbrush

extra + ordinary = extraordinary

A few compound words need hyphens between the words:

e.g. *I am an eight-year-old boy.*

1 In your notebook write as many compound words you can make
   using these words:

> any   every   some   no   one   body   where   thing   more

2 Write these animal words as compound word sums.
   bull + frog = bullfrog

> butterfly   earthworm   kingfisher   hammerhead shark
> grasshopper   rattlesnake   hippopotamus   jellyfish   sparrowhawk

(B) AZ Spelling strategies

If you don't know how to spell a word, you could:

- Use a phoneme frame to divide it up into its sounds like this:

t	i	g	er

- think of a similar word you know how to spell, for example *catch → match*
- think about prefixes and suffixes you already know.

Spell these words.

1

2

measure

3

nature

C AZ Alphabetical order

Dictionaries and other lists of words are often organised into alphabetical order. All the words beginning with A are first, followed by the words beginning with B, then C and so on.

1 Copy and complete the alphabet in your notebook:

a b __ d e __ __ h i j __ l m __ o __ q r __ __ u v __ x __ z

2 Copy and complete the alphabet in capital letters in your notebook:

__ B C __ E F G __ I J __ L __ __ O P Q __ S __ U __ W __ Y Z

3 Write these animal names in alphabetical order.

penguin   giraffe   bear   seal   fish   tiger   lion

D AZ Prefixes

A prefix is a group of letters added before a word. The prefix changes the word's meaning and makes a new word.

1 Look at this group of words:

unhappy   unfinished   unlucky   unfair   undone   unwell

What do you think the prefix *un* means?

2 Look at these words:

invisible   indirect   impossible   illegal   immeasurable
irresponsible   illegible   irrelevant

What do you think the prefix *in* means?

3 Match the beginnings and endings and write the spelling rules in your notebook.

   a The prefix in becomes im before   **1** words beginning with m or p.

   b The prefix in becomes il before   **2** words beginning with other letters.

   c The prefix in becomes ir before   **3** words beginning with r.

   d The prefix in is not changed before   **4** words beginning with l.

E AZ Suffixes

A suffix is a group of letters added after a word. Most suffixes change the kind of word it is.

1 The suffixes ful and less added to nouns make adjectives with opposite meanings (for example, thoughtful and thoughtless). Write the opposite of these adjectives by changing the suffix.

careful	harmless	thankful	doubtless
hopeful	painless	colourless	powerless

2 The suffix ment can change a verb into a noun (for example, *agree* → *agreement*).
The suffix ness can change an adjective into a noun (for example, *kind* → *kindness*).
Change these verbs and adjectives into nouns by adding a suffix.

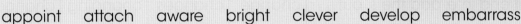

appoint   attach   aware   bright   clever   develop   embarrass

Term 2 Spelling activities

A [AZ] Spelling strategies

If you don't know how to spell a word, you could:

- use a phoneme frame to divide it up into its sounds
- think of similar word you know how to spell, for example *belief → brief*
- think about prefixes and suffixes you already know
- count the syllables and spell each syllable separately
- think about a spelling rule you already know.

Use some of the strategies to spell these words.

1  **2**  **3**  **4**

B [AZ] Spelling rules

Knowing rules about spelling can help you to make the right choices when you are writing. (But remember that English is a funny language and there are a few words that don't obey the rules.)

Rules for adding *s*, *ing* and *ed* to verbs

	Verb	+ s	+ ing	+ ed
Most verbs, just add the new ending	walk	walks	walking	walked
Verbs that end in *e*, add the *s*, but chop off the *e* before adding *ed* or *ing*	change	changes	changing	changed
Verbs with a short vowel followed by a single consonant, add the *s*, but double the consonant before adding *ing* or *ed*	clap	claps	clapping	clapped
Verbs that end in a consonant + *y*, change the *y* to an *i* and add *es*, *ng* or *ed*	try	tries	trying	tried

Copy and complete this table in your notebook.

Verb	+ s	+ ing	+ ed
push			pushed
	smiles		
carry			
			grinned
		hurrying	

Remember that plural means 'more than one'.

Rules for spelling plural nouns

Add s to most words (*chair → chairs*).

When nouns end in consonant + *y*, change the *y* to an *i* and add *es* (*story → stories*).

When nouns end in 'hissing' sounds (*sh, ch, s, ss, z, zz, x*) add *es* (*bus → buses*).

When nouns end in *fe* or a consonant + *f*, changes the *f* to a *v* and add *es* (*half → halves*).

Write the plurals of these nouns in your notebook.

baby	book	fox	house
knife	lady	wish	

 Prefixes

A prefix is a group of letters added before a word. The prefix changes the word's meaning and makes a new word.

1 Look at this group of words:

| disgrace | disappoint | disagree | discover | disappear |

What do you think the prefix *dis* means?

2 The prefix *mis* means 'wrong' or 'bad'. Add the prefix *mis* to the following words. What do they mean?

understand	take
behave	lead	place

D AZ Suffixes

A suffix is a group of letters added after a word. Most suffixes change the kind of word it is.

The suffix *ly* can change adjectives into adverbs (*quick → quickly*).

The suffix *ous* can change nouns into adjectives (*poison → poisonous*).

Sometimes you have to change the spelling of the word before you add the suffix (*infection → infectious*).

1 Add *ly* or *ous* to these words. What kind of word are the new words?

| busy | careful | caution | danger | easy | fame | funny | fury | kind | nerve |

2 Think about a spelling rule for adding suffixes.

Term 3 Spelling activities

A AZ Spelling strategies

If you don't know how to spell a word, you could:

- use a phoneme frame to divide it up into its sounds
- think of similar word you know how to spell, for example *belief → brief*
- think about prefixes and suffixes you already know
- count the syllables and spell each syllable separately
- think about a spelling rule you already know
- shut your eyes and 'see' the word on the inside of your eyelids
- use a mnemonic.

1 Draw calligrams in your notebook for two or these words.

catch	over	short	slow	tall

> Remember that a calligram makes the word into a picture.

2 Write a mnemonic for a word you find hard to remember.

B AZ Irregular verbs

You make the past tense of most verbs by adding *ed*.
But some irregular verbs have irregular past tense forms.

> Remember that a mnemonic is a saying that helps you to remember a spelling.

Match the verbs in the first box with their past tense forms in the second box. Write the pairs of words in your notebook.

begin	break	bring	buy	catch	come	do	give
have	hear	is	make	stand	think	throw	

caught	had	heard	came	made	broke	stood	was
bought	brought	thought	gave	began	threw	did	

C AZ Prefixes

A prefix is a group of letters added before a word. The prefix changes the word's meaning and makes a new word.

1 Look at this group of words:
   What do you think the prefix *re* means?

repeat	rebuild	return
reappear	renew	refresh

2 The prefix *sub* means 'under' or 'below', and the word *marine* means 'to do with the sea'. So a submarine is a vessel that goes underwater in the sea. Write definitions for these words in your notebook. You can look them up in a dictionary.

subway   submerge   subheading   subtract

D AZ Homonyms

Homonyms are words that have more than one meaning. Complete these pairs of sentences with homonyms.

1a People put their money in a … to keep it safe.

1b I like walking along the river … .

2a You … your hand from side to side when you say goodbye.

2b The surfer rode to the shore on a huge … .

3a You write … when you plan a piece of writing.

3b He couldn't play all the … because his piano was broken.

4a On clear nights the sky seems full of … .

4b The film … arrived at the awards ceremony.

5a Let's do something different for a … .

5b I gave her a ten-pound note and she gave me four pounds in … .

6a Please give me a … on my mobile number when you get in.

6b Her parents gave her a pretty pearl … for her birthday.

E AZ Spelling log

Keep a spelling log to help you learn how to spell difficult words.
Look at the spelling mistakes you make in your writing. If you spell a word incorrectly, write it correctly in your log. Identify the bit you found difficult and find other words with the same spelling pattern.

Copy this spelling log into your notebook and fill it in as you find words to learn.

Word	Tricky bit	Other words with the same spelling pattern		
learn	ear	early	earth	earn

Toolkit

Use these handy reminders to get on top of your grammar!

Different sorts of words

Nouns	Pronouns	Adjectives
Naming words for people, places and things: house flowers hope Maria London	Can be used instead of nouns: I you he she it we they his its mine	Describing words which tell you more about nouns: big pretty ordinary terrifying
Verbs	**Adverbs**	**Connectives**
Tell you what someone or something does, is or has: walk read like write have be take play	Give you more information about a verb – how, when or where the action takes place: slowly happily badly suddenly first then	Joining words that link sentences: and so but or when although because

Extra practice

Nouns

1 Find the nouns in the box and write them in your notebook.

> alphabet   bush   danced   horse   kindness   knife   sat   telephone   went

2 Now write the plurals of the nouns in question 1.
3 Write these sentences in your notebook using capital letters for the proper nouns.
   a ikram asked if he could borrow khalid's book.
   b Do you think that bianca and rafaela are sisters?
   c When he went to paris in november, jacques saw the eiffel tower.

> Proper nouns name people and places. They can also be the days of the week, the months of the year, the names of some buildings or the titles of books and films. Proper nouns begin with capital letters.

Pronouns

Rewrite these sentences in your notebook, using a pronoun instead of the underlined noun or noun phrase in each one.

1   <u>The camels</u> were tired of walking across the desert.
2   My name is Yao Meng. <u>Yao Meng</u> kicked the football into the goal.
3   Marcella said the book was <u>Marcella's</u>.
4   The boys played a match. <u>The boys</u> were happy because the boys won the match.
5   Jason and I are going to write a poem. <u>Jason and I</u> like writing poems.

Adjectives

Write a noun phrase in your notebook to describe each photo.

> Adjectives can come before the noun in a noun phrase (the terrifying tiger) or after it in a sentence (The tiger was terrifying).

Verbs

Verbs tell you what someone or something does, is or has.
A sentence must have a verb.
Verbs show tense – past (*I walked*), present (*I walk*) or future (*I will walk*).
For regular verbs, add ed to make the past tense.
Irregular verbs have different past tense forms.

> Check you know what verbs are!

1   Think of an interesting verb to complete each sentence and write the sentences in your notebook.
  a   The old man … down the street.
  b   The hungry cat … for its dinner.
  c   'Ouch!' … Winston.
  d   The wind made the leaves … .
  e   I … ice cream!

2 Decide which of the following are sentences. Write the sentences in your notebook.

   a The colourful fish.

   b They trudged slowly up the hill.

   c Can you read?

   d Mummy and Daddy.

   e Flowers grow in my garden.

   f My baby brother can't throw and catch a ball yet.

   g On the table.

3 Copy and complete the table in your notebook.

Verb	Past tense	Verb	Past tense
blow		read	
bring		run	
cook		sleep	
drink		smile	
eat		think	
enjoy		walk	
like		write	

Adverbs

Think of an adverb to complete each sentence and write the sentences in your notebook.

1 To make this snack, first peel the potato … .

2 He ran … out of the forest.

3 … the little girl met the wolf.

4 … it was getting dark.

5 … write your instructions.

Connectives

Join each pair of sentences with a word from the box. Write the new sentences in your notebook.

and	because	but
or	so	until	when

1 I am good at English. I am good at maths.

2 Giselle likes cats. She doesn't like dogs.

3 We like the weekends. We can play all day.

4 Vitor played the guitar. Someone stole it.

5 Do you like football? Do you like tennis?

Punctuation

Full stops	Capital letters	Commas
Mark the end of sentences:	Show the beginning of a sentence, proper nouns and titles:	Separate items in a list:
I love reading.	My best friend is Paula.	I need to buy apples, oranges, bananas and plums

Exclamation marks	Question marks	Speech marks
Indicate exclamations or commands:	Indicate questions:	Show words spoken in dialogue:
Help! There's a dragon!	Where are you going on holiday?	"I want to play hide and seek," she said.

Apostrophes

Show where two words have been joined together then shortened:

The fire isn't burning now.

Show possession – when someone has or owns something:

Arturo's aunt is Mrs Sabella.

> Punctuation adds meaning to a sentence. It helps us to read with expression and understanding.

Extra practice

Copy these sentences into your notebook, adding the punctuation.

1 im going out do you want to come with me asked grace
2 no i cant come ive got to finish my homework replied bianca

Text types

Fiction

Real-life stories
• These are stories about people like us.
• There is usually more than one character.
• There are real-life settings.
• The main character has a problem.
• Other characters help to solve the problem.
• There is a lot of dialogue to discuss the problem.
Myths, legends and fables
• These are very old stories that were told before they were written down.
• Myths and legends are set a long time ago. They can contain magical elements.
• Many cultures have their own myths and legends which help to explain the history of the people.
• Myths explain how something began.
• Legends are about heroes and heroines.
• Fables are often about animals and teach a lesson about life.
Adventure stories
• These are stories in which the main character or characters have an adventure.
• They can be real-life stories, stories about invented worlds or set in the past.
• The main characters are brave and solve problems.
• The language is exciting with lots of powerful verbs.
• There is often some dialogue.

Non-fiction

Instructions

- They tell you how to do something.
- The opening statement says what the instructions are for.
- There is often a section to tell you what you need to follow the instructions.
- They are written in order and are often numbered.
- Each instruction begins with a command verb or a sequencing word.
- There is very little descriptive language.

Letters

- They are written for many different reasons.
- The language matches the purpose (for example, friendly, business-like or complaining).
- Most letters begin with Dear and end with a finishing comment and a name.
- Postcards tell someone about a journey or holiday.

Information texts

- They give information about something.
- The main heading tells you what the information is about. Subheadings are used to show you what topic a paragraph or section is about.
- There is usually a contents page. There is often an index.
- The language is factual.
- There are photos, pictures and diagrams to give some of the information.
- There may be captions to tell you what is in a photo. There may be labels to show the different parts of a diagram or picture.

Poetry

Here are some more poems for you to read and enjoy.

A poem about the senses

Porridge is bubbling

Porridge is bubbling,
Bubbling hot,
Stir it round
And round in the pot.
The bubbles plip!
The bubbles plop!
It's ready to eat
All bubbling hot.

A poem with alliteration

Ten tom-toms

Ten tom-toms,
Timpani, too,
Ten tall tubas
And an old kazoo.

Ten trombones –
Give them a hand!
The sitting-standing-marching-running
Big Brass Band.

A calligram

THE SHAPE I'M IN

Wild as the rain

Come and see the shape I'm in

as a tale

Thin as a pin

strong as a train

I'm *this* and *that*

W i d e as a smile

I'm here   I'm there

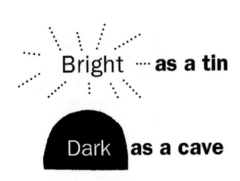

Bright ···· as a tin

Dark as a cave

I'm **eveRy**thing

&

Curved as a wave

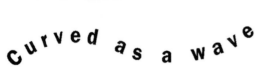
everywhere !

Limericks

A bald-headed man from Dundee
Lost his wig, in a wind, in a tree;
When he looked up and spied it,
A hen was inside it,
And it laid him an egg for his tea.

by Jack Ousbey

There was an old man on the Border,
Who lived in the utmost disorder;
He danced with the cat,
And made tea in his hat,
Which vexed all the folks on the Border.

There was an old man of Dumbree,
Who taught little owls to drink tea;
For he said "To eat mice
Is not proper or nice,"
That amiable man of Dumbree.